George William Sheldon

Recent ideals of American art

George William Sheldon

Recent ideals of American art

ISBN/EAN: 9783742892591

Manufactured in Europe, USA, Canada, Australia, Japa

Cover: Foto ©Thomas Meinert / pixelio.de

Manufactured and distributed by brebook publishing software
(www.brebook.com)

George William Sheldon

Recent ideals of American art

ONE HUNDRED AND SEVENTY-FIVE OIL PAINTINGS AND WATER COLORS
IN THE GALLERIES OF PRIVATE COLLECTORS,
REPRODUCED IN PARIS ON COPPER PLATES BY THE GOUPIL
PHOTOGRAVURE AND TYPOGRAVURE PROCESSES

TEXT BY
GEORGE WILLIAM SHELDON

NEW YORK AND LONDON
D. APPLETON AND COMPANY

LIST OF ILLUSTRATIONS.

PHOTOGRAVURES.

TYPOGRAVURES.

LIST OF ILLUSTRATIONS FOR THE SUPPLEMENT.

Frederick Dielman &

FREDERICK DIELMAN : *The Mus-Players.*

RECENT IDEALS OF AMERICAN ART

FOR fresh subtilties and cunning mediums of technique the American artist of the present decade has a profound respect. His predecessor had a fondness for addressing himself to matters of sentimentality, of animation in design, of innocuous story-telling, but he himself can draw and paint soundly and is learned in the practice of his art. Sixty years ago— or, to be precise, on the 30th of July, 1828—in an article on certain deficiencies in the library of the British Museum, the London *Athenæum* complained that the institution contained no copy of Buffon's works. "We are well aware," it said, "that Buffon's works are not considered to possess a scientific character, and in his natural history of so well known an animal as the sheep, Lord Kaimes assures us that scarcely one fact is correct. Yet in all books on zoölogy Buffon's is referred to, and there can be no question that what he wanted in *scientific accuracy he made up for by elegance and eloquence*, qualities which modern naturalists require as much to study as the scientific systems of Linnæus, Cuvier, Jussieu, or Latreille, if they are desirous of rescuing their favorite science from the unpopularity into which repulsive scientific systems have thrown it."

This interesting extract describes with exactness the position of the earlier American artist: he valued "elegance and eloquence" more than sound drawing and sound painting, and his friends considered popularity as the supreme test of merit.

To-day the American artist who can draw and paint soundly has a chance of selling his work at good prices. Perhaps twenty citizens of New York city alone are forming collections exclusively of American paintings; and not one of them puts much store by mere "elegance and eloquence." The landscapes of men like Inness, Wyant, Tryon, Murphy, Davis, and Bolton Jones, find purchasers as soon as they are put on the market, and much of the time of these artists is occupied in filling orders. A clever prizeman, like Ulrich, is sent to Europe by one collector—Mr. W. T. Evans—who gives him an order for an important picture, and pays him in installments in advance, so that he can live meanwhile upon it. A business man, like Mr. Altman, bids five thousand dollars at auction for a snow-scene by Bliss Baker, and adds the picture to his collection of one hundred examples of American art, not that he may sell it, but that he may enjoy it. The demand for good work is sustained and increasing, while the canvases of the sentimentalists were never before worth so little. The private collector makes his purchases, not "to encourage American art," as was often urged as a duty twenty-five years ago, but to please his tastes and to invest his money. Some of our connoisseurs, to be sure, still profess a lack of interest in the productions of the native studio, but, when their attention is seriously directed to its later triumphs, their commendation is usually prompt.

This improved condition of affairs is due primarily to the importation into the United States of the best works of the best modern painters, leading to a dissatisfaction with much that we ourselves had produced. A few of our artists, notably Mr. Inness, and Mr. Wyant, and Mr. Swain Gifford, had all along been shedding the light of their example as accomplished technicians; and their influence upon the present condition of art in this country should never be overlooked, particularly as all three of them have lifted up their voices in the public prints as well. But the re-enforcement that came from the pictures of Millet, Corot, Rousseau,

Diaz, Dupré, and other contemporaneous masters was, after all, the notable means of reform. The worth of their work, recognized first of all on the Continent of Europe, led our principal art-dealers to bring to these shores the best specimens

Louis Moeller : *The News of the Day.*

obtainable, and these specimens were in many instances so good that many a private gentleman's gallery in the United States contains more valuable and representative examples of the Fontainebleau school than does the Louvre itself. This is one of the first things that strikes the American who visits the Louvre to-day, and it speaks volumes   America has, indeed, done better than did Venice at the

height of her glory: for the Bride of the Adriatic imported a vast quantity of
very poor art; and, at the sack of Constantinople, her generals left behind them
pictures and statues of great beauty and value, esteeming chiefly a multitude of
superstitious relics which, at great pains, were transported home.

The ease and speed with which the trip to Europe is now accomplished have
done much for the improvement of American art. Many artists spend each summer abroad, and to no artist does a sea-voyage seem a great undertaking. So
great has been the influx of foreigners into the École des Beaux-Arts in Paris that
the French students have felt compelled to protest against it in the newspapers.
In 1886 a pamphlet entitled "De l'Envahissement de l'École des Beaux-Arts par les
Étrangers" was published, containing extracts from French journals, and a general
history of the case. The *République Française* said that the influx had arrived at
such a point that in a number of the ateliers of the École des Beaux-Arts the
Americans and the English were in a majority, and won certain prizes consisting
of sums of money, although the Frenchmen who had founded them never intended
that they should fall into the hands of strangers. "Yet things have now come
to such a pass that strangers enjoy a better chance than we of obtaining them."
The Paris *Nation* declared that it was high time that this state of things should
cease; that the École des Beaux-Arts was created to aid the development of art
in France and not among strangers; and the French pupils in architecture wrote
a letter thanking the editor for his action. Moreover, the French pupils as a body
issued an address in which they declared that "the Americans, who come by
thousands to enter our schools, now that they have painters and a few sculptors,
lay a prohibitive tariff on the importation of our works of art"; and Mr. L. W.
Hawkins, an English artist of fourteen years' residence in France, wrote a letter
to the *Figaro* in which he advised vigorous retaliatory measures in view of the
American duty of thirty-three per cent. Nevertheless, our young Americans continue to avail themselves of the very great advantages of the École des Beaux-Arts,
and have made an impression also in the art-schools of Munich. Even after
returning home to settle down they sometimes pull up stakes and go back to
France, as did that brilliant painter, Mr. Frank M. Boggs, who has since been
awarded medals and much praise.

The establishment of the American Art Galleries, with their four annual prizes
of two thousand dollars each, and their eight or ten annual prizes of gold medals
for paintings, has done a great deal to foster American art. From their studios in
France and Germany, our young artists send twice a year to the public exhibitions
in those galleries their choicest new works, many of which, as in the case of

Raphael's cartoons of the Acts of the Apostles, show how much their authors progress in the art of composition; and so agreeable are the galleries as places of exhibition that the public crowds them. The National Academy itself has awakened to some extent from the sleepiness of its routine, has made improvements in its old galleries, and now offers several prizes annually, the latest being those founded by Mr. Thomas B. Clarke, Mr. Norman W. Dodge, and Mr. W. T. Evans. The annual exhibitions of the Society of American Artists, which originated in a protest against the favoritism in hanging, and the methods of technique of the Academicians, afford other opportunities for making pictures known. The Metropolitan Museum of Art

CARL MARR : *The Gossips.*

and the Art Students' League in New York, the Boston Museum of Fine Arts, the Philadelphia Academy, the Corcoran Art Gallery, the Peabody Institute, and kindred institutions hold annual exhibitions of native art; and so, in fact, do the principal cities of the great West. The erection of commodious and handsome studio buildings in New York city, especially in Fifty-fifth Street, has provided the rapidly increasing number of artists with suitable accommodations for work ; and hardly is such an edifice finished before its rooms are engaged by bright young men starting out in their careers, after thorough training in the technique of their profession in the Continental schools. Some of the leading social clubs, notably the Century and the Union League Clubs of New York, hold monthly exhibitions, sometimes exclusively of American works

Meantime the wonderful progress in the reproductive arts—wood-engraving, etching, photogravure, and phototype in its various forms—has increased the demand for pictures by ministering more generally to it, and has encouraged the artist by the fidelity and rapidity with which his work can multiply itself. Nothing in the history of the fine arts has been more interesting than the brilliant episode of American wood-engraving; but in some respects the process of photogravure on copper has superior attractions for the painter, because it reproduces with exactness his drawing, and shows the deep brilliancy of etching in its blacks. If any reader will contrast the results in Mr. Hamerton's *Portfolio* in 1877, in such photogravures as those of the street-scene by Mr. Frederick Walker, and the "Divided Attention" by Mr. George H. Boughton, with the results presented in this volume, he will become convinced of the great growth of the process during the last ten years.

With all this advance in the condition of the American artist it may be objected that socially, at least, he is not of more importance than he was during the last generation; and that in England, for example, his life would be more agreeable than in his own appreciative land. But let us quote some testimony from a capable observer, Mr. P. G. Hamerton: "People are beginning now to estimate an artist very much by his way of living. If his brush can keep up a fine establishment, he is considered a great painter; if he lives moderately and economically, he is not thought to be very successful in his profession. The consequence is, that some of those who earn the most money are the most hardly pressed by the necessity for earning, and do the most rapid work." How different from Fra Angelico, watching the Venetian skies (and painting them, too) from the window of his modest room in the Dominican convent! Let us be thankful that no such cruel environment as that of the successful English artist has yet chilled the aspiration and warped the ideal of his American brother.

Subtilty of design and extreme delicacy of touch caused Mr. Walter Blackman's picture of "Contemplation" to be greatly admired, a few months ago, in the galleries of the American Art Association. As in France, so in America, works of this class show great national progress. The demand for them has been active of recent years, while the demand for grand historical compositions and religious paintings has been small. In France the government has been too poor to decorate the walls of the churches and the other public monuments with anything like the liberality of earlier days; and in this country the government has never decorated the churches and but rarely has provided for the employment of painters in public edifices or in memorial works. Mr. Blackman, long a student in Paris, whence he sent to New York this beautiful picture, has entered into the spirit

of the truest contemporary idealism, and has given to the world a conception worthy of standing side by side with those in the gallery of the poets. Thoroughly modern in type, and rich in the veracity of the model, this interesting and speaking woman is a representative of traits that Shakespeare loved to depict; and by the aid of an accomplished technique, which finds itself at home in the presence of poetic ideas, Mr. Blackman has been able to express himself clearly and tersely, wasting no words and at a loss for none. Shall we say that the gentle creature

RICHARD CREIFFTS : *Playing Checkers.*

to whom he introduces us is, like Rosalind, filled with all graces, or, like Cleopatra, nobly majestic, or endowed with sad Lucretia's modesty, or, like Miranda, perfect and peerless, created of every creature's best? It matters little. She has the power to interest and please, and she stirs the imagination.

Mr. Blackman has gradually found his way through a course of *genre* subjects to the ideal heads, of which the "Contemplation" is the most successful. His serious and protracted study in Gérôme's atelier has only given him the use of the tools of his profession, without reducing him to the necessity of copying Gérôme's compositions, or echoing Gérôme's style. None of his friends can fail to be pleased with the conception and execution of the fascinating picture here reproduced as a representative of his talent. It is original to a high degree, and it is worthy of successors. The American who can go to Paris and stay there as long as Mr. Blackman has, without degenerating into a mere imitator of French artists, seems proof against the most facile and the most perilous of temptations; and the artist who can charm us with the ideal deserves the admiration that has never been refused him.

The history of American art will not omit the name of Moran. The three brothers, Thomas, Peter, and Edward, have contributed valuable works to the annual exhibitions for many years, and are represented in private collections in the principal cities—Thomas Moran by his transcripts of Rocky Mountain scenery, in Turneresque style; Peter Moran by his etchings (of which a remarkably comprehensive collection was recently placed on public exhibition in the gallery of Mr. Frederick Keppel); and Edward Moran by his marines. The ladies of the family have also achieved distinction as executants with the brush, and an entire volume of good size might easily be filled with descriptions of pictures painted or etched by the Morans. Percy Moran, a son of Edward Moran, has come into prominence in recent years as a painter of *genre*, and the subject which here represents him is as successful as any to which he has ever set his name. In the presence of his accomplished drawing and coloring many of our elder artists seem weak. Like them he has a fine natural sensibility and a cultivated taste, but, unlike them, he knows how to paint. These three ladies of an elder day, chatting over their tea-cups, in the picture entitled "Gossip," are as interesting as the celebrities of the court of Marie Antoinette, and the dresses they wear, the carpet they tread on, and the furniture they use, are alike dainty. They do not suggest the model, but seem to have come down to us from a beautiful civilization, ready to step out of the frame when they leave the little mahogany table. With vivacities of local tones, Mr. Percy Moran is, at the same time, a true colorist; with charming softness of outlines, the softness is never that of indecision. His brush does not hesitate; his hand does not grope. Not too careful of details to sacrifice the value of wholes, not too attentive to form to appeal directly to the heart, he pursues the wise middle path which is the path of the poets. He has a fondness for comedy, for the "society drama," and he selects salient points without insisting too much upon them; and we may almost say of his types what Mr. Lowell has said of the types of Cervantes, that they are not so much taken from

F. S. Church : *Mermaid and Sea-Wolf.*

life as informed with it; not the matter-of-fact work of a detective's watchfulness, products of a quick eye and a faithful memory, but the true children of the imaginative faculty, from which all the dregs of observation and memory have been distilled away, leaving only what is elementary and universal. The reader will not fail to appreciate the brilliancy of the Goupil photogravure after this subject.

In the little village of Auvers-sur-Oise, at about an hour's distance from Paris by rail, Mr. Charles Sprague Pearce, of Boston, has established himself for the purpose of painting impressions from Nature that have already made him famous; and how faithfully he reflects the pastoral spirit of his surroundings is known at least to those who, like the writer of these lines, have visited Auvers-sur-Oise, and strolled along its banks or rowed upon its waters. The tall, slender poplars, in the background of the picture, are extremely characteristic—one often sees them in that region—and scarcely less so are the massed acacias of the middle distance; while as for the young peasant-women, seated on the bank, you will find them, any fair summer's day, helping their fathers and brothers in the fields. "On the Bank of the Brook," recently hung in Mr. Knoedler's gallery, New York city, is one of several, by the same artist, that we have been permitted to reproduce for this book of ideals of American art. Like many other landscape-painters in France, Mr. Pearce has a glass studio attached to his principal studio, and in it he is able to paint summer landscapes in all weathers. The plants and grasses of his foregrounds, which demand a treatment more or less detailed, are to be found under the glass roof, and the peasant models needed for the composition take their places in the midst of them. Sometimes these models, that they may be available whenever wanted, are employed as domestic servants in artists' houses.

By a happy suggestion or intuition, Mr. Pearce has recently been painting his pictures in a gray tone, which serves to prevent them from being at once compared by everybody with Millet's, and gives them an air of distinction much needed by an artist who, after Millet and Jules Breton, has chosen to depict the lineaments and the occupations of the French peasant-woman. People do not say of Pearce's compositions, "They look like Millet's"; and it is primarily and most obviously to their gray tone that their independence is due. Still, the surroundings of Auvers-sur-Oise are not absolutely similar to those of Barbizon, although when Millet opened the back gate of his garden, in the latter village, he saw a vast extent of harvest-fields, less rolling than those of Auvers, and bounded on one side by the rocks and towering beeches of the forest of Fontainebleau. This picture of the two peasant-girls seated "On the Bank of the Brook"—or perhaps we might say on the bank of the Oise itself—is one in which the painter, having infused his intellect with the sense of beauty, has striven to charm the spectator. He has no message to tell about the botany of the plants, nor the texture of the garments; his aim is not to instruct but to delight, and his influence stirs us like the sight of the beautiful fields of Brittany.

After fifteen years of study and travel in foreign parts, Mr. Frederick A. Bridgman brought to the United States, in the spring of 1881, a collection of three hundred oil-pictures and studies, so diverse in subject as to surprise the spectator who had known him only through his larger and finished works. It was evident, however, that the scenery and people of Algiers and Morocco most invited and longest detained him—the Bedouin Arab, with swarthy face half concealed by an overhanging white cloth; the Moor, with embroidered jacket and snowy turban; the Moorish woman, her bright eyes alone of all her features uncovered; Algerian girls, in full, short trousers, gauzy chemisettes, and sleeveless pink jackets. "The women," writes a traveler in Algiers, "wore silk jackets, stiff with gold embroidery, as were their crimson girdles. A striped gauze scarf hung down in petticoat-fashion over wide trousers terminating at the knee; bracelets, necklaces, and rings encircled arms, throats, and fingers. From the gay silk handkerchiefs on their heads to the small, pointed, gold-embroidered shoes into which their henna-stained feet were thrust, the bridal-party showed no lack of zeal in personal adornment. The bride, seated in a cross-legged attitude, motionless as a statue, in the center of a narrow stage extending from wall to

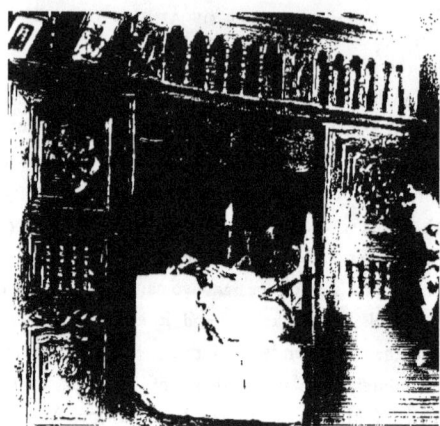

wall, showed a youthful face glittering with gold-paper, stuck in patches on the chin and cheeks, and in broad strips upon the forehead, above eyebrows joined by a black streak across the nose; her head a mass of sparkling jewelry; her bust bare but for a chemisette of filmy gauze and numerous strings of pearl; her

CHARLES SPRAGUE PEARCE : A Cup of Tea.

hands, partly blackened and ladened with rings, extended flat on either knee, and her eyes fixed in an unwinking stare"—these are the things that Bridgman likes to depict. And if we examine the subjects that he has chosen since this exhibition in New York, we shall find that with Northern Africa still his brush has been concerned. In 1882, he exhibits "The Fountain at the Mosque," with spirited studies of horses; in 1883, "La Cigale"; in 1884, a domestic interior at Cairo; in 1887, "On the Terrasses, Algiers"—the same reminiscences of Oriental life that had engaged his brush during his first visit to Algiers, fifteen years earlier. And these subjects—as in the present instance—he treats, not in the spirit of one who raises the standard of revolt and inaugurates a new epoch, but rather after an ideal more or less conventional which Delacroix has set up. There is an Algerian interior by Delacroix in the Louvre, "Femmes d'Alger dans leur Appartement," where the figures in dress, in color, and in disposition of lines, suggest very sharply one source of the inspiration of such charming pictures as the "Oriental Interior" and the "Woman and Rose," the American painter depending at the same time upon the direct observation of Nature. His master, Gérôme, has also influenced him, particularly in his earlier works, as, for instance, in the "Fête in the Palace of Rameses," which has kinship with Gérôme's famous "L'Almée." But there can be no question that to-day Mr. Bridgman's sympathies are with Delacroix rather than with Gérôme, nor does Gérôme usually retain the riper discipleship of his pupils.

No subject has been treated oftener by painters of *genre* than that of maternal affection; and, in the history of religious art, no subject is less infrequent than that of the Virgin Mother and her divine child. Of recent years, M. Edouard Frère has interpreted with great popular success the sentiment of Mr. Jones's picture, but the American's handling of the theme is less mannered than that of the Frenchman. Mr. Jones, a brother of the landscape-painter, Bolton Jones— the two artists occupying the same studio in the Sherwood Building, New York city—has a sympathetic apprehension of the possibilities of his subject, and there are circumstances which combine to give to his work an imaginative character. He is a teacher in one of our art-schools, and a regular exhibitor at the National Academy; and when we speak of his imagination we use the term in the Ruskinian sense, holding that the virtue of that faculty resides in the fact that it reaches a more essential truth than is seen on the surface of things, and that this reaching is through intuition and intensity of gaze, rather than by reasoning.

Mr. Jones is one of the younger painters of our promising *genre* school, and, like his brother, has enjoyed a course of liberal education in France. Nothing could

be simpler than the manner in which he has conceived his idea; nothing could be
more truly single than his method of expressing it.   All the facts in the picture are

RIDGWAY KNIGHT : *Resting.*

homogeneous. The mind of the spectator is diverted neither to the right hand nor
to the left. His sympathy with the lowly young mother is complete. He feels

that the artist was created to paint such subjects, just as the Spaniards were created to play on the guitar, and as the English were created for exploits in commerce. Mr. E. L. Weeks's picture of the "East Indian Horsemen," admirable in many things, is most admirable in its affluence of sunshine, which radiates in every direction, giving tone to the brilliant hues that it embraces, and reflecting a yellow warmth into the recess where the figures are grouped. The greatest of modern writers on art has said that, while Claude and Cuyp painted the sunshine, Turner alone painted the sun-color; that, previous to Turner, the colorists in general, feeling that no other than yellow sunshine was imitable, refused it, and painted in twilight when the color was full. "Therefore," he argues, "from the imperfect colorists—from Cuyp, Claude, Both, Wilson—we get deceptive effects of sunshine; never from the Venetians, from Rubens, Reynolds, or Velazquez. From these we get only conventional substitutions for it, Rubens being especially daring in frankness of symbol. Turner, however, as a landscape-painter, had to represent sunshine of one kind or another. He went steadily through the subdued golden chord, and painted Cuyp's favorite effect, 'sun rising through vapor,' for many a weary year. But this was not enough for him. He must paint the sun in his strength, the sun *not* rising through vapor. If you glance at that Apollo slaying the Python, you will see there are rose-color and blue on the clouds, as well as gold" (alas! to-day, both the rose-color and the blue have, like the gold, disappeared in blackness); "and, if then you turn to the Apollo in the 'Ulysses and Polyphemus,' whose horses are rising above the horizon, you see he is not rising through vapor, but above it; gaining somewhat of a victory over vapor, it appears. Herein rests, not merely the question of the great right or wrong in Turner's life, but the question of the right or wrong of all painting. Nay, on this issue hangs the nobleness of painting as an art altogether, for it is distinctively the art of coloring." And who among our American artists, more than Weeks himself, has illustrated by his work his belief in the beauty and nobleness of pure sunshine? Or who among them more deserves that such a passage should be quoted in connection with his pictures? Look at that fine composition, the "Promenade of a Rajah," the black horse with gold trappings, his royal rider in a costume of gold brocade of Benares, and a turban and shoes of gold lace; the bearer, in front, with black coat embroidered in gold, with red turban, and with silver staff; the gayly-equipped cavalry-escort behind; the pretty Nautch-girls in the balcony, resplendent in color; the damsel at the door with her scarlet skirt, her transparent muslin drapery, and her bare brown skin; the house itself, with its projecting windows of finely-wrought stone-work pale brown in color; the mountebank, with his white-bearded monkey squatting on the sidewalk;

the deep-blue sky. Here, again, it is sunshine that the painter has painted—pure
sunshine, brightening, mellowing, softening
whatever it touches.

Or, in the "Arrival of a Rajah at the
Palace of Amber," see how the sunshine
deals with the embroidered trappings of
the kneeling elephant, with the silver
wands of the bearers, with the brilliant
silks of the ladies of the Zenana, and with
the beautiful façade of the palace—one
of the finest structures in India, better
situated than the Alhambra, to which it
is a perfect parallel in architectural style
and importance. See how the highly-
polished serpentine of the pavilion on the
left reflects warm light from the sunlit
pavement. The great gateway behind is
a mass of carved stone, painted in ara-

CHARLES SPRAGUE PEARCE A Reverie.

besques, and inlaid, while above the inner arch appears a plaque of alabaster on
which a divinity has been enameled in black and gold, near the three latticed
windows of red sandstone that disclose the blue sky. The general tone is yellow,
both from local color and reflected light; but in the "Departure for a Hunt,"
owned by the Corcoran Gallery, and showing some trained cheetahs at the palace
of Futtehpore in the time of the Emperor Akbar, in the sixteenth century, the
general tone of the architecture is a pale red, with warm reflected lights from
the glaring pavement, against a deep flat blue sky. Again, we see a subject
chosen, not for its literary significance, but for its chromatic values, as the sunshine discovers them in the richly-carved Hindoo work of the pavilion on the
left, called the House of Beerbul, after a prime minister of Akbar, in the wall
of the great palace behind it, in the purple-velvet trappings, embroidered with
gold, of the elephant, and in the figures of the two cheetahs, trained like dogs
to hunt gazelles and deer, and still pursuing the vocation of their predecessors
of two hundred years ago. One of the most unique places in India is this
abandoned capital, Futtehpore, full of magnificent specimens of architectural genius.

For a gray sky, but luminous still, and strong local color, the "Cashmere
Travelers passing through a Street in Delhi" is notable. The portico of the temple

shows finely-wrought open-work of clay-colored stone. One of the dancing-girls of the sacred edifice appears on the balcony with a large red fan having a frilled border. The rider of the white horse wears a yellow embroidered coat. The man walking by his side has a red printed cotton caftan, and a light-blue cashmere shawl. In strange contrast with the pretty women above him is the ugly, squatting fakir, his cotton drapery a pale-orange color, and his skin the tone of the gray dust with which he has powdered himself. Mr. Weeks has learned that, to express India, one must paint the hideous and the grotesque side by side with the beautiful; but he attaches himself to the purest traditions of classic art by his systematic and conscientious search for beauty in tone and in line. In addition to the " East Indian Horsemen," we shall reproduce some of these other examples of Mr. Weeks's brush.

The " Moro-Players " of Mr. Frederick Dielman, which introduces the illustrations inserted in the text, is one of the best known of recent American genre paintings. It belongs to the private collection of Mr. John Herriman, of the Union League Club in New York city, and was conspicuous in the remarkable exhibition of American works organized in the gallery of the Club on the 11th of March, 1886. Mr. Dielman, the artist, though a native of Hanover, Germany, has resided in this country since early childhood, and is an American of the Americans. After graduation at Calvert College, in Baltimore, he was a draughtsman of the corps of United States Engineers at Fortress Monroe, and next a student of painting in Munich. When the bright young painters who found reason to protest against the methods of the National Academy of Design resolved to organize the Society of American Artists, first known as the American Art Association, Mr. Dielman was recognized as a leader; but so broad was the scope of his art, and so popular was the painter among his comrades, that he soon found himself elected a member of the National Academy itself. The Etching Club, the Salmagundi Club, and the Water-Color Society have enrolled him among their members, and some of the most beautiful and artistic editions of the works of American poets reflect his services as an illustrator. His simplicity and directness were never seen to more advantage than in the faces and attitudes of the two street Arabs in the " Moro-Players." These boys do not pose; their claim to our attention is based upon no intrigue. They are set forth by a man who despises all tricks and all mannerisms, and the day is not likely to come when the owner of this painting will see its value decrease.

Following Mr. Dielman's picture is the " Prelude " of Mr. Charles Sprague Pearce, who is represented also by the sturdy young peasant whose kind face

illumines the cover of the first section of this book, and by the "Cup of Tea," the "Reverie," and the "Shepherdess." Each of these beautiful compositions presents clearly the poetic quality of Mr. Pearce's genius, and we note particularly the success with which the textures of the Japanese girl in the "Cup of Tea" have been reproduced by the Goupil process.

EASTMAN JOHNSON : *The Justice of the Peace.*

Mr. Louis Moeller's "The News of the Day" is painted with a fidelity to detail worthy of Meissonier, and it is worth mentioning that his methods do not permit him to make use of the camera. Every bit of still-life in the picture, as well as the figure of the sitter, is a piece of free-hand drawing, and not a tracing on a photograph. Mr. Moeller has few rivals among the promising *genre* painters of this country. In his own sphere he already is a leader. Mr. Richard Creifelds, the author of "Playing Checkers," is a native of New York. He studied art in Munich for about seven years, in company with Dielman, Shirlaw, Chase, and Louis Moeller. Mr. Benjamin Altman owns two of his pictures, "The Veterans," a group of three chess-players, and "Mate in Three Moves," a solitary chess-player at the board. Mr. Henry T. Chapman, Jr., has two study-heads, one entitled "The Professor" and the other "The Pensioner." The subject reproduced here is owned by Mr. Thomas B. Clarke, by whose permission, also, "The News of the Day," by Mr. Moeller, has been reproduced. Mr. Carl Marr's "Gossips," a reminiscence of New England life, took a prize of two thousand dollars in the American Art-Galleries, and was purchased by Mr. George I. Seney, who has permitted its reproduction for this work, and has recently presented it to the Metropolitan Museum of Art. The subjects treated by Mr. Ridgway Knight— a Philadelphian living in France—show no suggestion of the influence of his teacher, Gleyre, whose fondness was for representations of Venus, Diana, Daphnis and Chloe, of Ruth, Boaz, and the Twelve Apostles, of bathing Romans and Nubian women. Nor does Meissonier, who, after Gleyre's death, became the master of the young American, seem to have left an impression upon him. In "Sunshine," a canvas recently hanging in the gallery of M. Knoedler & Co., we have a characteristic example. A peasant-woman, in a harvest-field of Brittany, lies resting on her elbow, gazing with pride and affection upon her infant child, whose face she has protected from the sun by a large umbrella. The husband and father we may suppose to be among the workers near by, and, when her baby is older, the young wife will take her place by his side, to earn her bread by the sweat of her brow. Just now, maternal duties are paramount, and the sunshine around her is but a type of the gladness within her. A peasant-woman of the same class appears in the typogravure illustration in the text, standing beside a large net used in crab-fishing. Her thoughts, however, are elsewhere, though not clouded. Mr. Knight does not see the sadness of French peasant-life, but its gladness. He is neither a Millet nor a Zola. The spirit of his work is akin to the spirit of Mr. Eastman Johnson's work, and the "Justice of the Peace," by the latter artist, is a transcript of rural American life which Mr. Knight himself

would have liked to attempt had he been painting on this side of the water. Such subjects as the "Old Kentucky Home," the "Old Stage-Coach," the "Husking-Bee," and the "Cranberry-Harvest," to which Mr. Johnson has signed his name, commend themselves to Mr. Knight with equal force. In the "Justice of the Peace" the artist has caught and fixed a type rather than painted the portrait of a model, and has done it so well that one feels that it never need be done again. Here is the New England squire, sterling in his integrity, honest in his adminis-

BURR H. NICHOLLS : *Near Central Park.*

tration of the law, resolute, self-satisfied, domineering, public-spirited. The moment that Mr. Johnson showed him to the solid men of New York at a Union League Club exhibition, their response was decided and approving. Many of them were from New England themselves, and recognized an old type; the rest felt that the type was there as strongly as if they had seen the original examples. Mr. Burr H. Nicholls's study of the shanty "Near Central Park" represents a rapidly-vanishing phase of our metropolitan civilization. Masons and carpenters are now taking possession of the lots in the neighborhood of the park, and large stone and brick dwellings, with all the modern improvements, will soon occupy the sites so long and so modestly held by the squatters. Mr. Nicholls, like Mr. Knight and Mr. Johnson, has striven to paint what he saw with his own eyes—to interest the spectator with the simplest annals of the poor; and it must be confessed that the sprightliness of his humor adds much to the pleasure of the recital. When one recalls the days of conventional forms and unemotional figures, the opposition that Giotto was compelled to overcome in his effort to make intelligent to the average mind the pictorial presentation of Biblical events; when one looks back upon much more recent times, and remembers the struggles of the Classicists and Romanticists, the subject chosen by Mr. Nicholls seems adapted to designate an epoch of its own. A long distance have we journeyed from those studios of the Renaissance where, to be orthodox, the artist must embody in the form of a Venus his conception of beauty. Mr. F. S. Church's fancy has produced a style entirely his own. "The Mermaid and the Sea-Wolf" is unlike any other subject in this collection, and, as a play of pleasing tones, has also a place apart. The genius of Mr. Church is now fully recognized, and his paintings are eagerly sought by the most enlightened collectors. To Mr. William T. Evans we are indebted for permission to reproduce this striking picture. Mr. Henry Mosler's "Prodigal's Return," the Brittany mother of the prodigal having died too soon to receive his confession, is the only American picture in the Luxembourg Gallery. The officers of that institution have allowed this copy to be made for this book.

ALEXANDER HARRISON : *Sunlight on the Sea.*

II.

J. CARROLL BECKWITH : *A Portrait.*

CONSPICUOUS among the influences that have produced the present epoch of American art is the active interest taken by certain successful business men in the fortunes of the young American painters, who, after a course of study in Paris or Munich, have returned home to practice their profession. To such aspiring artists the new environment is often peculiarly uncongenial. The stimulus of an art-atmosphere, as Parisians understand the phrase, is denied them. Buyers do not frequent their studios. Neither the methods nor the aims of art are understood by the general public, and even the critics themselves are at variance on questions of theory and practice. What the late Matthew Arnold used to call the literary influence of academies—the advantage accruing from the presence of a recognized authority in matters of taste—does not exist: there is in this country no institution corresponding to the French Academy, and there never has been. Nor have we that serious and higher instruction of the people, which, according to M. Renan, is an effect of the advanced culture of certain classes, and the absence of which, if the same critic may be believed, is expiated by intellectual mediocrity, vulgarity of manners, a superficial spirit, and a lack of general intelligence. Suppose, now, in such a state of things, be it actual or presumed, the presence of a business man, who, with some knowledge of art and much fondness for it, sets himself to the work of gathering for himself a private collection of American paintings, and encouraging his prosperous friends to perform a similar service for themselves. He feels that, if our young artists on returning from Europe find in their own land a market for foreign work only, they have a right to be discouraged. He believes that as good work as any can be produced in the United States, and that, if these artists are given a start, they will reach the goal in triumph. To those who have shown themselves to be the possessors of genius, he thinks that society owes the duty of keeping them from starvation. Such a patron of art is Mr. Thomas B. Clarke, of New York city, who owns the largest private collection of American paintings in the United States. He has seen every one of his pictures painted or signed, so that their authenticity never can be questioned. The first of them was bought in 1874, in the studio of Mr. Wakeman Holberton, the subject being a collection of trout just thrown upon a bank, slimy and dripping. A trout-fisher himself, the truth of the delineation pleased him, and, as at that time many forged coins were selling, he resolved to avoid the auction-rooms and to frequent the studios. He was no such bigot as to believe that he was collecting the great art-works of the world, but he did foresee that our native art could become promising only by being patronized, and with this conviction he proceeded, on all suitable occasions, to interest his friends, at the club and on 'Change, in the attractiveness of American paintings as an investment. His first full appreciation of landscape art came from the works and the words of George Inness, of whom he owns at least a dozen examples, and whose "Gray, Lowering Day," a summer idyl of meadow, trees, and brook, he still remembers as a source of consolation in an hour of sharp personal bereavement. No artist ever had a more earnest or useful friend. It has for years been Mr. Clarke's delight to take buyers to Inness's studio and introduce them to its treasures. His contributions to the monthly art-exhibitions of the leading clubs have been repeated and numerous, and to the Academy Exhibition of 1888 he sent George Inness's "September Afternoon," which was the star landscape; Mowbray's "Evening Breeze," which was the star figure-piece; Curran's "Breezy Day," which was the star *genre* landscape; and Shirlaw's "Cronies," A. P. Ryder's "Christ appearing to Mary," Winslow Homer's "Eight Bells," and F. M. Boggs's "January Tow," all of them important and characteristic.

Among the American artists who treat pastoral subjects, Mr. Ridgway Knight and Mr. Charles Sprague Pearce now occupy a foremost place. For a number of years they have been painting in France—Mr. Knight at Poissy, where he has recently purchased the fine old château of the town; and Mr. Pearce at Auvers-sur-Oise. Each has made a study of the Brittany peasant-woman in her relations to the landscape that environs her, each has sought the essential and found it, and each has remained steadfast to the truth without degrading himself with the trivialities of prose. The first person who compared painting and poetry with each other, says Lessing in his famous treatise, "The Laocoön," was a man of fine feeling, who perceived that these arts produced upon him a similar effect; and it

H. BOLTON JONES : *Willows.*

is the poetry of women's lives in the fields of Brittany that Mr. Knight and Mr. Pearce offer us, each of them in his own manner, and each without servility to the great contemporaneous master in the same department, Jules Breton, of Courrières. These American painters have gone to France, one of them from Philadelphia, the other from Boston, and, attracted by the same rustic scenes that inspire the pencil of Jules Breton, have, in their own way and by their own genius, wrought poems that delight and refresh. Some years ago a friend of Jules Breton, on the occasion of this artist's exhibition of his "Evening in the Hamlets of Finistère," at the Paris *Salon*, gathered into a little volume the principal criticisms that had been published concerning that beautiful picture; and it is not a little curious how many of the praises there sung are applicable, or promise to be applicable, to the best work of Knight and Pearce. Jules Breton's picture, says one critic, possesses a depth and sweetness that appeal to the ignorant as well as to the cultivated. Everything, observes another, is rendered with simplicity and fidelity, and with the discretion and strength that characterize the talent of the poet-artist. The composition abounds, declares a third, in realistic sentiment and grand poetry. A fourth finds it as much the work of a poet as of a painter. "What a profound regard for art, what respect for form, what love of effect!" exclaims another. "It is a quiet poem, which reveals on the part of the artist an extensive study of rustic life and an ingenuous belief in the power of art to elevate the figures of the humblest by the mirage of style. What clearness of expression and honesty of *mise en œuvre!* Profound is that art which knows how to make itself forgotten. These faces are attractive because they are profoundly human. What a subtile charm in the features of the young women! What repose in Nature! How everything sees and thinks! One would love to isolate himself before this canvas, where the spirit of the master irresistibly attracts."

Such words as these, from the current art-criticism of France, indicate at least the direction in which Knight and Pearce are growing, and many of them might justly be used with reference to the charming pictures signed by them in this portfolio. Concerning the work of Mr. Knight, however, one exception needs to be taken. He places a higher value upon the French peasant than does either Jules Breton or Millet. "The French peasant," says M. Charles Clément, in the *Journal des Débats,* "leads a sad, hard lot. He is at his work before daybreak, and does not leave it until nightfall. From the first moment of his life until the latest he does the same things over and over again, revolving in the same circle of monotonous occupation. He always sees the same people, the same fields, the same skies. Bound to the soil by regular and continued labor, and generally alone, the peasant becomes absorbed in his own reflections. This contemplative and silent existence develops in him certain habits which are reflected in his entire person, and which give him a simplicity and grandeur of character that M. Breton has treated with wonderful power." Akin to this estimate, only more somber still, is the declaration of Jean François Millet: "O sadness of field and wood! I should miss too much in not seeing you"—the field and the wood seeming sad because the peasant was so. But to the American painter the aspect is very much less dreary. "These peasants," said Mr. Knight a few months ago to the present writer, "are as happy and contented as any similar class in the world. They all save money, and are small capitalists and investors. They enjoy

life. They work hard, to be sure, but plenty of people do that. They love their native soil. In their hours of ease they have countless diversions; and the women know how to be merry even in their hours of toil." Mr. Knight's

HENRY P. SMITH : *Along the River.*

presentation of the French peasantry in his oil-paintings shows no sympathy with Millet's presentation of them, and none with Jules Breton's, in so far as Jules Breton sees only their "sad, hard lot." And, as for the American's profundity, his interpretation of character seems more nearly fundamental than that of his French contemporaries. In the summer of 1887 the present writer was riding in an open carriage between Melun and Barbizon, the home of Millet. It was an August day, and the sun was broiling. We overtook on the road a peasant-woman, also bound for Barbizon, six miles distant—a servant, she said, in a country-house which we had just passed, and on her way to spend Sunday afternoon with her mother and sister. One of the ladies in the carriage asked her to take a vacant seat, the heat was so intense. She accepted, with great ease of manner, the offered kindness; but, although we had pitied her, she seemed neither tired nor sad. She had never heard of Millet, she said; nor, from his paintings, could we believe that Millet had ever heard of her. As we reached Barbizon, her younger sister, a sunny-faced girl of sixteen, was in the street to meet her. Their greeting and general demeanor were merry and joyful. The reader will see them both in Mr. Knight's *Salon* pictures (here reproduced) "In the Vineyard" and "In October," and certainly one of them in "At the Well" and "In Winter." Whatever M. Charles Clément may think of them, they do not, in their own estimation, lead "a sad, hard lot."

In one of those delightful letters written by Henri Regnault to his father, during his travels in Spain, the artist says: "Our great difficulty has been to persuade the gypsies to sit to us. For a long time they would only consent to tell our fortunes, and then went away; but yesterday, at last, we induced three to pass the day at the atelier. We made a study of them, and they are splendid. One of them is expecting to become a mother. I am to be godfather to the baby, which is to come into the world in the month of January. I should like to assist at a gypsy festival, now I am one of the family. Our three friends of to-day promised to bring two more to-morrow. I hope they will give us letters of introduction to their relations in Andalusia, so that we may be well received there next year. We went, a day or two ago, to see the future mother, under the guidance of the honest fellow, her husband, who showed us the way to the little suburb outside Madrid inhabited exclusively by gypsies. It was night. We entered a long, one-storied house, divided into several compartments; each family occupies one. A charcoal-fire was on the floor in the middle of the room. On one side were the mattresses on which they sleep. All the occupants sat in a circle warming themselves, the children perfectly naked. The donkeys passed freely backward and forward, eating the straw that was scattered about." On another occasion Regnault describes a visit to one of the wine-shops of Madrid—" little dens frequented by the common people and *toreros*. Sit down with us and take what these courteous fellows, with their bright-colored handkerchiefs and embroidered jackets, offer so hospitably. They pass their glasses, and, after you have done them the honor of drinking, they will put it to their lips, too. Listen to Lola while she sings, with her soft, mellow contralto, one or two gypsy dirges, or a love-song, with its long-drawn sighs and monotonous rhythm, to which the guitar makes such an exquisite accompaniment. Then, ' *Hóla! hóla! hóla!* ' they jump up, clapping their hands. A handsome *picador* begins to dance, showing his white teeth, and throwing himself from side to side, while he holds the silk scarf tied around his loins. And, when that is over, to bed! for we have work to do to-morrow." In such a spirit has Mr. Knight studied the peasant-life of Normandy, and, if his private letters could be printed before his departure from these mundane scenes, many a passage of similar import might be found. The literature of art-life does not contain paragraphs more truly descriptive of the

manner in which Mr. Knight has possessed himself of the subjects which he paints. Throughout Normandy he is a familiar figure in the field and in the cottage. A hundred times has he been called upon to act as godfather to the children of his models, and, whenever one of them gets married, she is sure to receive from Mr. Knight a handsome present in gold. His habit in this regard is well known among them, and he is able to choose his models—how charming they are!— from a class which usually are not willing to serve in such a capacity.

With his disdain of facile effects, and his ease in mastering difficulties, Mr. Marcius-Simons is always interesting; and "The Young Lulli" strikes the note of a sincere and personal interpretation. It is not the first time that pictorial art has chosen for a subject this incident in the life of the great French composer of the time of Louis XIV, but Mr. Simons places the scene, not in the kitchen— where most painters place it—but in an abandoned bosquet near the reservoir,

CHARLES SPRAGUE PEARCE : *With her Sheep.*

where were situated the dependences of the palace. It will be remembered that in childhood Lulli, a Florentine peasant-lad, was sent to France to act as buffoon to Madame de Montpensier; but, on his arrival at her house, the lady was so displeased with his lack of personal beauty that she sent him to live with the servants in the kitchen. Here he amused his humble listeners with improvisations on the violin, the strains of which one day came to the ears of his distinguished mistress, and so charmed her that she proceeded to discover their source. Her surprise was as great as her admiration, and she at once took the trouble to present young Lulli to the king, an act which laid the foundations of his success as a composer. Mr. Simons has chosen the moment when Madame de Montpensier first hears the boy playing on his violin, unconscious of the presence of his distinguished listener and future patron. As Socrates once quaintly observed, "The good and evil qualities of the soul may be represented in the figure of man by painting."

We are indebted to a Paris friend of Mr. Marcius-Simons for some interesting biographical memoranda: The artist was born in New York city, but was brought to France in infancy for his health. He is now (1888) twenty-five years old, though looking scarcely more than eighteen, and has visited his native land but once since his departure from it. Slight in figure, nervous in manner, delicate in health, with regular features and an aristocratic expression, speaking English brokenly, but using it in preference to any other tongue, he is an enthusiastic admirer of his own land, and a firm believer in its artistic future. Much of his earlier life was spent in Spain and Italy, but his academic education was pursued at the celebrated Vaugirard College in Paris, under the direction of the Jesuits. So successful was he in his studies that he received the unusual permission to study art also during his collegiate course; and, when the distinguished painter Vibert had resolved to receive some pupils, the youngest of the group was Marcius-Simons, who had been recommended by the celebrated Detaille. The American's health was severely tried by the resolute ambition which made him simultaneously a collegian and an art-student; and, as if still further to test it, M. Vibert invited him to become a member of his family after the regular term of his atelier had closed, thus giving him an extraordinary opportunity for mastering the art that he loved. For no teacher was ever wiser in method or kinder in spirit. Instead of endeavoring to graft his pupil's style upon his own, he permitted it to grow freely by its own roots in its own soil, with the result that, while no critic ever accused Mr. Simons of being an imitator of M. Vibert, there is, perhaps, no young American in Paris who has acquired so much of his teacher's dexterity and certainty of touch. The right tools, and how best to use them—this he learned thoroughly, and under the most favorable auspices, of his accomplished and beloved master. To Louis Leloir, also, he was much indebted, particularly

RIDGWAY KNIGHT : *In Winter.*

for hints for water-color painting; and, indeed, it may be said that most of Mr. Marcius-Simons's professional friends have been artists much older than himself, who seem to have been attracted toward him in the first instance by the extraordinary friendliness displayed by M. Vibert. His tastes are as far from those of the Bohemians as from those of the madding crowd, and when he lays down his brush his favorite companion is a book. Our readers, we are sure, will not be displeased at the announcement that other works by Mr. Marcius-Simons, in addition to the brilliant "Young Lulli," will be reproduced among these "Ideals of American Art"; nor will they be reluctant to echo the hope of his friends that his physical strength may long be equal to the task of setting forth on canvas the very beautiful products of his thought and imagination.

A recent English writer has lamented that beauty is just the quality most difficult to find in modern French art; that it is not to be seen in their portraits of women and children, nor in their nude figures of a semi-classical type; that Carolus Duran's pictures are those rather of a costume than of a person; that Bouguereau prefers the small waists of the Parisian *modiste* to the more simple line from shoulder to hip of the Greek statues; that even the work of Meissonier, admirable though it is for subtile expression and inimitable finish, makes little effort after beauty, and possesses no imaginative or poetic quality. In all the parts of the artist's work which can be learned, the French school, he admits, has a mastery. It excels, in other words, in its academic qualities—in the power to draw correctly; to put a scene in perspective and represent distance by changes in size and strength of tone; to group masses together so that each helps the effect of the others; to make the picture tell its story frankly and lucidly. But, in all the parts of the artist's work that depend upon his individual genius—in conveying the sense of beauty, in appreciating form as distinct from mere correct drawing, in fineness of handling, and in the eye for color—the French school is distinctly inferior to the English school.

Now, if this estimate were a true one, every well-wisher of the contemporaneous American school, whose exploits are commemorated in this portfolio, would find cause for discouragement. It is to the French, rather than to the English, that our young Americans look for their inspiration, outside of Nature herself; and it is from the French, rather than from the English, that they have taken the precepts and the principles of their art. Certainly, the sense of beauty, which this English critic laments the absence of in French painting, is not absent from the work of our young Americans. It abounds in Mr. Weeks's "East Indian Dancer" and the "Promenade of the Rajah," in Mr. Hartwich's "Resting at the Stile," in Mr. Marcius-Simons's "Young Lulli," and in such characteristic examples of Mr. Knight as "In October," "At the Well," "In the Vineyard," "In Winter," "Returning from the Garden," and "A Mourning"—all of them here reproduced. To deny its presence in many of the nymphs of Bouguereau, and in the Napoleons

of Meissonier, in many of the peasants of Jules Breton, and in the early mornings
of Corot, is absurd.   One's patriotism carries him too far when it blinds him to

RIDGWAY KNIGHT : *Returning from the Garden.*

the existence in French art of compositions as poetic and touching as the English
Millais's "Huguenot Lovers"; and a chief source of congratulation, on the part
of believers in our new American school, is the fact that, while so many of our

rising young artists have gone to France to learn matters of academic training, so few of them have learned to despise the presentation of poetic beauty which confronts them in the greatest of the French masters.

The fear expressed by the late President Arthur, in one of his messages to Congress, that our import duties of thirty per cent upon works of art might result in "the practical exclusion of our painters and sculptors from the rich fields for observation, study, and labor, which they have hitherto enjoyed," has not been justified. Although much anxiety has been displayed by various European governments, and especially by the Government of Italy, no formal measures of retaliation have been instituted. This is due, doubtless, to the generally understood fact that American artists themselves are, as a body, opposed to the present discrimination against the productions of their brothers abroad. In 1883 no less than three hundred native artists signed a petition in favor of the free admission of works of art into the ports of the United States. The next year the Union League Club of New York city proceeded systematically to ascertain the sentiments of American artists on this subject, and undertook to procure an expression of opinion from every artist, institution, and teacher of art in the United States, excluding from the plan all amateurs, dealers, or purchasers. It asked for signatures to a petition to Congress setting forth the facts that high duties on the importation of works of art can be justified only on the ground that such objects are manufactures and need protection; that painting, sculpture, and the kindred arts, are not manufactures in any commercial sense, but means of education and cultivation; and that improvement in artistic taste promotes industry by increasing the skill and elevating the aims of our workmen, and by creating a demand for such improvements as add to the beauty and convenience of our homes, our dress, and everything that gives pleasure to the mind or comfort to the body. The petition reminded Congress that ours is the only nation in the civilized world that levies heavy duties to keep works of art outside of its borders; that the law of 1883, by which the duties were raised from ten to thirty per cent, was not called for by artists, was not advocated by the press, was not demanded by the people; and that, as a measure of financial policy, it had already proved a failure, since it had restricted trade and diminished the public revenue.

In response to this request, nearly one thousand letters were received, all of them in favor of the petition. The feeling, indeed, was practically unanimous throughout the studios of the Union that free trade in art-works was necessary for the national prosperity; and the views expressed by M. Gérôme, the distinguished painter, in a letter to a friend in New York, were also those of American artists

themselves. Said M. Gérôme: "In the huge budget of the United States the sum arising from duties on pictures is but as a drop of water to the ocean. But there is a moral aspect to this question. It is in France and Germany, but more especially

CHARLES SPRAGUE PEARCE : *Resting*.

in France, that your young painters have been taught. We have given them this teaching gratuitously. They have been treated precisely like our own subjects in the state schools. Consequently, it is to foreigners that they owe what they know. Is it just to treat the works of these foreign artists, these educators, with such severity?" To see what could be done, M. Gérôme called a meeting of American and French painters in Paris, and found that the Americans were as dissatisfied as the Frenchmen. A memorial was addressed by the former artists to Congress, deprecating a measure so damaging to the interests of their Continental brothers. The Americans, continues M. Gérôme, "thoroughly understood their obligations to us; how well they had always been treated by us; how they were admitted to the École des Beaux-Arts on the same footing as French students; how at the annual exhibitions they enjoyed the same rights and privileges as our native artists; and how they received prizes and good positions in the *Salon* when they deserved

them. . . . They did everything in their power to induce Congress to recon-
sider this outrageous measure, and, if they did not succeed, it is not to be laid
to their charge. People will, one day, say: 'It was at the close of the nineteenth
century, in the full flush of civilization, that the strange, odd idea cropped up of
likening the products of the mind to sardines in oil and to smoked hams. All
over the world works of art were duty free. In one country alone were they
saddled with an excessive tax, and that country was the youngest, the greatest,
and the wealthiest of nations!'"

That the establishment of the annual prize exhibition of the American Art
Association has exerted a wholesome influence upon the rising school of national
painters no competent observer is likely to deny. This interesting event took
place in the summer of 1884, when a number of gentlemen well known as
patrons or connoisseurs of art created a fund for the awarding of four prizes of
twenty-five hundred dollars each, and ten gold medals worth one hundred dollars
each, to fourteen of the most successful contributors to an exhibition of American
art, held in the new galleries of the American Art Association in the city of
New York in the spring of the following year. Among the subscribers to the
fund were W. T. Walters, Charles A. Dana, Cornelius Vanderbilt, Henry G. Marquand, John Taylor Johnston, William H. Vanderbilt, Heber R. Bishop, L. Z.
Leiter, Samuel M. Barlow, Frederick Billings, H. O. Havemeyer, and J. Abner
Harper, and their subscriptions were paid directly into the vaults of the United
States Trust Company, subject to the order of the jury of award, which was
selected from the number of the subscribers themselves. In order that the pictures
which won prizes should be placed where they could be seen to advantage, it
was determined to present them to the principal art museums of the United
States—to such institutions as the Metropolitan Museum of New York, the Corcoran
Gallery of Washington, the Museum of Fine Arts in Boston, and the Pennsylvania
Academy of Fine Arts in Philadelphia; and all American artists, whether domiciled
in this country or abroad, were invited to send specimens of their skill. At the
opening of the first exhibition, the public and the press were surprised at the beauty
and the importance of the result, and it was generally believed that no display
of American art at once so valuable and so promising had ever been made, even
the National Academy Exhibition being dwarfed by contrast. The successful competitors for the four principal prizes of twenty-five hundred dollars each were
Mr. Alexander Harrison, "Le Crépuscule"; Mr. Henry Mosler, "The Last Sacra-
ment"; Mr. R. Swain Gifford, "Near the Coast"; and Mr. Frank M. Boggs,
"A Rough Day: Entrance to the Harbor of Honfleur." The next year, under

similar auspices, prizes of two thousand dollars each were awarded to Mr. F. D.
Millet, for his "At the Inn"; Mr. C. F. Ulrich, for his "Glass-Blowers of
Murano"; Mr. C. P. Grayson, for his "Midday Dreams"; and Mr. E. E.
Simmons, for his "Mother and Child." At the third Prize-Fund Exhibition, prizes
of two thousand dollars each were won by Mr. Charles H. Davis and Mr.
Edward Gay, both landscape-painters; and at the fourth Prize-Fund Exhibition a
single prize of two thousand dollars was given to Mr. J. Alden Weir for an
interior with figures of a mother and child—said to be the wife and daughter of
the artist. It would be incorrect to assume that in all cases the distribution of
these prizes was considered absolutely just and felicitous. Some complaints found
their way into the newspapers, and many protests fell from the lips of disappointed exhibitors and their friends. But universal satisfaction in such cases is

RIDGWAY KNIGHT : *A Mourning.*

not to be expected, and perhaps not to be desired. The fact of significance in
connection with the present subject is the indisputable stimulus of the Prize-Fund
Exhibitions to the growth of native art. Mr. C. F. Ulrich's "Glass-Blowers of

Murano" (Italy) served to extend his reputation. It is now hanging in one of the large western galleries of the Metropolitan Museum of Art, and is reproduced here through the kindness of the officers of that thriving institution. The "Sunlight on the Sea" resembles in composition the "Crépuscule" of Mr. Alexander Harrison, though the latter picture is a moonlight. Mr. W. H. Fuller is the owner of the "Sunlight on the Sea," a subject as purely a marine as ever was painted, seeking no adventitious aid from the presence of ships, bathers, buoys, wharves, or storm. Not even a bird has been introduced to define the plane of the water. The wave-drawing shows unusual skill, and there is a keen appreciation of the qualities that distinguish moonlight from weakened sunlight.

A few weeks before the first awards of the Prize-Fund Exhibitions were announced, a company of artists and their friends assembled at the rooms of the Art Students' League in New York city to witness the presentation of the first scholarship of the Hallgarten-Harper Fund. This scholarship provided its holder with the means for a two-years' course of art-study in Europe, and was awarded to Mr. Ernest L. Major, a pupil of the Art Students' League, by a jury consisting of Messrs. T. W. Dewing, Walter Shirlaw, Abbot H. Thayer, J. Alden Weir, Olin L. Warner, W. M. Chase, R. Swain Gifford, F. D. Millet, and Augustus St. Gaudens. The writer of these lines well remembers the singular interest of the occasion—the heartiness of the congratulations extended to young Mr. Major by his fellow-artists, on his reception of the diploma of scholarship, and the far-reaching import of the simple ceremony itself as interpreted by the speakers to the audience. "This event," said Mr. F. D. Millet, in a carefully prepared address, "has more significance than any other I could name, both as distinguishing the real from the apparent interest in art, and in marking the beginning of a new era in our art education. In a country like France, where, since the establishment of the Academy of Fine Arts by Louis XIV in 1648, the study of the profession has been esteemed as honorable, and has been recognized as of public importance, there has been insensibly developed an instinct for and an appreciation of art which can only be the result of generations of artistic culture. It is this wide and distinctly apparent sympathy with the fine arts that largely distinguishes society abroad from society at home. It is the single-minded devotion to the profession common to the artists and the students, joined with their inherited and their acquired taste for art, which makes association with them so valuable to an American, and which, in fact, largely contributes to that art-atmosphere which is so salutary and stimulating to all who enjoy its influence. Every student knows the kind and the quality of the influence which accompanies association

with his fellow-students. By the side of this influence, the individual assistance of the professor, however useful and necessary, is of comparatively small importance. In the art-schools abroad the American student finds his comrades among those to whom the idea of art is as familiar as the alphabet. His intimate association with them supplies, in a great measure, the deficiencies of his early training. He not only readily assimilates the art-ideas, which to the foreign student are almost second nature, but he unconsciously acquires that respect for the profession and that devotion to it which is one of the elements of success in its practice. This alone would make European study of the greatest value to him. But the greatest of all the advantages of foreign travel and study is the priceless

privilege of seeking artistic stimulus and inspiration at the very fountain-head of all modern art, the works of the old masters and the masterpieces of ancient art." The next day, the New York *Evening Post* observed that the awarding of the Hallgarten-Harper scholarship marked "a memorable phase in the art education of America, not only as being the first recognition in this shape of the advantages of foreign study of art, but as demonstrating in a brilliant manner the value of the Art Students' League, whose pupil the prize-holder is. Study at home is indispensable in its way, but art is a collection of traditions and experiences which no man's life is long enough to

FRANK FOWLER : *Anticipation.*

accumulate without aid, and this, in the unwisdom of our laws, and the worthlessness of the action of our official institutions, will be long in crossing the Atlantic to us. Our young men have the same need to go abroad to perfect their education in art as in medicine, music, or archæology, and the directors of the League have shown that they recognize both the home need and the European need in their system of instruction."

While the position here assumed is that of the great majority of American artists and critics, it can not be questioned that an influential minority do not sympathize with it at all. "America for the Americans" is their watchword; "let the painter study art in his own land, and paint the subjects that suggest themselves around him." The advantages of a foreign training are, in the minds of these remonstrants, offset by the disadvantages; and, if an artist is to preserve his originality, and retain the power frankly and freely to express himself, he must decline to subject his brush to the inspiration of European masters and European scenes. To us it seems that every argument advanced against a course of foreign study for an American artist might be advanced with equal propriety against the acquisition of what is known as a liberal education. Moreover, experience does not teach that the American artist who stays at home is always original in his subjects or his methods. The first demand upon the painter, as upon the writer, is that he should have something to say, and the next is that he should say it simply and directly. A knowledge of the classics does not make an American write worse; and a knowledge of the best that has been thought and done in the studios does not make an American paint worse. Originality, after all, is the rarest of gifts, and the most truly original artists of the present day are those who have made themselves proficient in the science of the schools. We, therefore, hail with pleasure the Americans who, like Ridgway Knight, Charles Sprague Pearce, E. L. Weeks, and F. A. Bridgman, are sending home the masterpieces which they have painted abroad. These masterpieces are as truly American as the most cherished productions of our "Hudson River School." Mr. Knight's series of Normandy idyls—his "At the Well," with its pretty story of peasant love-making; his "In the Vineyard," with its vine-clad hill, its shapely women, its happy children, and its central pair of not-too-daring lovers; his simple story of the "Halt" beside the stone wall in the midst of the peaceful landscape; his "In October," with the merry harvesters—these pictorial transcripts, all of them, depict rural France as an American sees it. Mr. Weeks's fresh chapters of Oriental poetry and prose—his "East Indian Dancer," swinging her rounded arms and swaying her lithe form before the young sovereign, the ministers, and the admiring slaves, seated in the court of a palace whose architecture is as delicate and beautiful as that of the Alhambra; his "Promenade of the Rajah" in the streets of a city of India before the doors of a temple, from whose balconies fair priestesses or choristers are bending—are the records of an American's impressions in the distant East. Mr. Ulrich's "Glass-Blowers" takes us, under the tutelage of an American, to the factories of Murano; and Mr. Hartwich's "Resting at the Stile," under similar auspices, to fields of France, where rest a stalwart reaper and her child. Mr. Dana's "Light and Labor," with the fine illumination of its sunshine through sea-mists that soon will envelop coast, draught-horse, and laborer alike; Mr. H. P. Smith's cottage homes "Along the River"; Mr. Boughton's "Shepherd's Idyl"—who is vested with authority to declare that these children

of the artists' faith and fancy are less "American" than the "Willows" of Mr. Bolton Jones, the "Portrait" of Mr. Carroll Beckwith, or the "Anticipation" of Mr. Frank Fowler? It is in the direct personal significance of all these works that their true value lies, and this significance has an American quality, because the artists are American.

The scholarship that bears the name of the late Mr. Julius Hallgarten is not the only souvenir of that merchant's devotion to the interests of American art. By a deed of trust to the National Academy of Design, he has endowed prizes of three hundred, two hundred, and one hundred dollars, to be awarded to the painters of the three best pictures in oil-colors at each annual exhibition of that

W. P. W. DANA : *Light and Labor.*

institution. His directions for the management of this trust were as follows: All works will be considered in competition which have been painted in the United States by American citizens under thirty-five years of age, and which have not before been publicly exhibited in the city or vicinity of New York; no competitor may take two prizes, nor a prize of the same class a second time; the awards will be made by a vote by ballot of all the exhibitors of the season, at a meeting held for the purpose during the third or fourth week of the exhibition; each artist will be entitled to one vote at each ballot, specifying his choice for each one of the three prizes, and each prize will be awarded to the painting receiving the highest number of votes for that prize, but no work will be entitled to the prize unless at least fifty of the exhibitors vote at the ballot, and the canvas receive one third of all the votes cast; any prize not awarded on or before the third ballot will not be awarded at the time, but will be reserved for and added to the prize or prizes of the following year. The first meeting of exhibitors to award the Hallgarten prizes was held at the National Academy on the 22d of April, 1885, and the successful competitors were Mr. Harry Chase, who received three hundred dollars for a marine entitled "New York Harbor"; Mr. J. Francis Murphy, who received two hundred dollars for a landscape entitled "Tints of a Vanished Past"; and Mr. Dennis M. Bunker, who received one hundred dollars for a figure-piece entitled "A Bohemian." Since the year 1885 these prizes have been regularly awarded at each of the spring exhibitions at the Academy.

The same number of the catalogue of that institution which recorded the establishment of these Hallgarten prizes made the following announcement concerning another prize: "Mr. Thomas B. Clarke, of New York, has generously provided a prize of three hundred dollars to be awarded yearly to the best American figure-composition painted in the United States and shown at the annual exhibition. This prize will be offered at the same time and place, and awarded in the same general manner, as the Hallgarten prizes. Academicians are not eligible." The first recipient of the Clarke prize was Mr. Francis C. Jones, whose picture entitled "Exchanging Confidences," and representing an old farmer and a child at a breakfast-table, now belongs to Mr. Clarke's private collection. Mr. Ridgway Knight's presentation of the saucy but delightful French peasant-girl, "Tired," might easily have been a winner, had it not gone to another exhibition.

RIDGWAY KNIGHT : Tired.

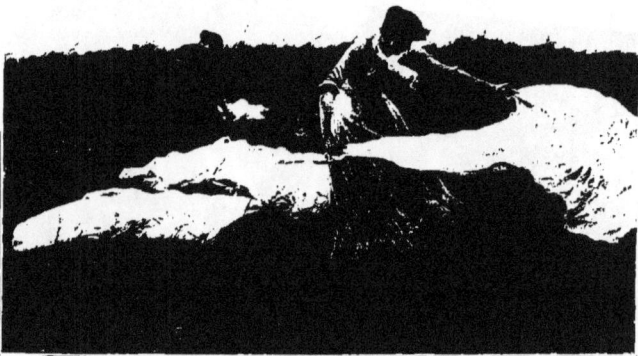

CHARLES C. CURRAN : *A Breezy Day.*

III.

WALTER BLACKMAN : *Expectation.*

THE true triumphs of the present period of American art are set forth to advantage by recalling the characteristics of its earlier period; and nowhere have these characteristics been more acutely depicted than in a critical review of the annual exhibition of the National Academy, which appeared in the year 1855 in the columns of *The Crayon*, at that time the leading art-journal of the United States. "It is evident," said the reviewer, "that we need not talk very largely of an American school of art, nor look for any very strong indications of a national and peculiar greatness. Such as there are, however, are mainly found in landscape, which, from the temperament and tendencies of the people, we imagine will be, as in England, the leading branch of art for many years to come. But the chief deficiency in our landscape is a want of invention. Our pictorial scenery is generally poor in incident and deficient in the thoughtful recognition of the minuter facts of Nature. When the first impression is over, the mind ceases to find further interest in it. There are blank spaces—breadth without meaning—masses of paint which seem as if the artist, at that particular juncture, had forgotten the minutiæ which Nature presents in infinite store. He can not recall the forms. In other words, he can not invent. And so he leaves smearings of the brush which, though they may be right as far as composition and color are concerned, have nothing of individual truth in them, and are, indeed, nothing to the mind." This, in the judgment of the reviewer, was all wrong, for no picture was complete until every inch of the canvas was full of thought. He did not consider it necessary to point out instances of this defect; few pictures in the exhibition could be studied without finding it. Frederick E. Church was the most remarkable and complete exception. His invention was uncommonly fine; wherever he touched his pencil to the canvas, there was evidence of some positive recollection of Nature; and this faculty of his was one of the most extraordinary things in modern art. The direct cause of poverty of invention was the habit of making broad sketches without particular reference to details—mere studies of color and effect. The artists' minds, accustomed to regard only in masses the objects received by the eye, ceased to notice that these objects existed individually. The true method of study was to take small portions of scenes, to explore perfectly and with the most insatiable curiosity every object presented, and to define it with the carefulness of a topographer. Young artists should never sketch, but always study. The interest of the exhibition was mainly in portrait and landscape works, there being in American art very little that was really excellent in figure. Following upon this great deficiency in landscape art was the tendency to rush to the grandiose, the striving for that which was striking and palpable. The true poetry of art consisted not in being able to grasp large themes so much as in elevating simple ones to beauty and impressiveness. The American artist rushed to huge mountains and mighty cataracts, to flaming sunsets and wild effects, to the occasional ejaculations of Nature by which she varies her tranquil and serene labors. An elm was at least as beautiful as a palm, and a ruined tree as picturesque as a ruined tower. The abundance of subjects for the pencil had itself a tendency to make painters superficial in their selection. A third deficiency was a want of subtilty of treatment. As a general thing, the landscape-painters were palpable in their treatment, depending too much on the subject presented by the picture, and not caring enough for the way in which it was presented.

Now, what are the facts of the case to-day? Can it be said with truth that we have no American school; that our art is notable almost exclusively

in the department of landscape; that we have very little of real excellence in
figure-painting; that even our landscapes are belittled by a want of invention,
and, therefore, are "nothing to the mind" of the intelligent spectator; that
Frederick E. Church's canvases, admirable in many respects though they are,
represent the exercise of "a faculty which is one of the most extraordinary
things in modern art"; that the prevailing tendency of landscape-painters is to
rush to the grandiose—to mighty mountains, blazing sunsets, and exceptional
scenic effects; and that subtilty of treatment is foreign to their pencils? To all

ALFRED C. HOWLAND : *They're Coming.*

these questions a distinct negative must be given. Our artists to-day are as
proficient in the figure as in landscape, and we have created in landscape a
young and promising school, represented by David W. Tryon, Charles H. Davis,
J. Francis Murphy, and others, whose expressions of their impressions of Nature
are poetry itself, tender, true, and sometimes as stirring as that of the great men
of the Fontainebleau school whom all of them so deeply reverence. The spirit
of these Americans is the spirit of these Frenchmen, and instead of trying to
excite our wonder with transcripts of Yosemite or Niagara—with grand cañons,
terrible torrents, enormous pines—they choose themes as simple as Mr. Alfred C.

Howland's "They're Coming," or Mr. Ridgway Knight's "Going to the Wash-House."

Enter the schools of the Art Students' League, for example, and what do you find? The League is a voluntary association of young men and women for the study of art. After an existence of only a few years, it is able to spend more than fifteen thousand dollars a year for rooms, for teachers, and for models. Not content with the advantages offered by the National Academy of Design, it proposed to infuse into its course of instruction something of the best contemporaneous European spirit, by engaging the services of young artists like Kenyon Cox, Walter Shirlaw, William M. Chase, J. Alden Weir, T. W. Dewing, Thomas Eakins, H. Siddons Mowbray, William Sartain, and J. Carroll Beckwith, all of them recently students in France or Germany. The Academy, of course, soon felt the influence of its new and more ardent rival, and made additions to its own corps of instructors; but, although the cost of tuition to the pupil was much less than in the ateliers of the League, the latter institution soon outgrew the former in the eyes of the most promising and ambitious of the novices. At its annual meeting in 1886, it reported that the number of classes was seventeen, and the number of students four hundred and seventy-five—an increase of sixty-six over the number enrolled the previous year. There were a class in composition and a class in anatomy, a class in perspective and a class in sketching; two classes for the study of the antique, two for the study of the head, two in painting, and five for the study of the living nude model. The genius of the École des Beaux Arts seemed to have presided over the place, and it was generally conceded that the instruction given was similar in mode, if not in measure, to that of the leading art-schools of Paris and Munich. How long this voluntary association of pupils will hold together can not be predicted; the opportunities of the situation may be short-lived at best; but the results already obtained, especially the demonstration of the usefulness of the democratic spirit in organizations for art-study, will commend themselves to the attention of the historian. And what are the modern names most frequently on the lips of these teachers and pupils? None others than those of Corot, of Millet, and of Rousseau. Listen to the addresses delivered on anniversary occasions by speakers selected by the students. How strong the contrast between the spirit of such discourses and the spirit of the discourses which the pupils of the National Academy were accustomed to hear a quarter of a century ago! I cite an interesting and suggestive example in an extract from a speech of Mr. E. H. Blashfield—one of whose fine allegorical compositions has been reproduced for this portfolio—delivered on the 11th of January, 1885, at a

reception given in New York city by the students of the Gotham Art School.
"All good art," said the speaker, "should be decorative. The Greek sculptor
working at his temple, Michael Angelo painting in the chapel of the Popes in
Rome, were creating some of the noblest things that exist upon the earth, yet
both of them belong to what we now call the school of decorative art. And so
all of us here are artists, whether we work on marble, canvas, leather, wood, or
what not, and I hope that all our work will prove decorative. As to the

RIDGWAY KNIGHT : *Going to the Wash-House.*

necessity of art, people have told you time and again that art is a luxury—a
thing that one must be educated up to; a thing to be paid for by the rich man
—the great railroad man or the banker. So, in its more elaborate form it is,
because to produce it a man must take a long time for training, and another
long time for the execution of the work, and, if living is dear, he must be well
paid for it; but, in another and a broader sense, art is not a luxury, but a
necessity. Much more than that, the instinct for art is one of the very first
instincts of man. Thousands upon thousands of years ago, before history began,

when oceans stood where there is now dry land, and continents where there are now oceans, there were artists. If we could look back with our modern eyes, we should see a cave with its mouth blocked by fragments of rock to keep out the beasts—the tigers as big as oxen, and the cave-bears bigger than oxen. Inside, by the light of the fire, a man is carving, upon the horn handle of his hunting-knife or upon his stone hatchet, a rude representation of a mammoth or a deer. There you have him, the artist. He saw the mammoth, hunted him, and perhaps was hunted by him; then, when he had returned home, he tried to make a representation of him. Once, in one of our Western forts on the plains, a drunken Indian woman was shut up in the guard-house; she broke into the postmaster's desk, and, while the regiment was on dress-parade, she appeared on the ground, her body stuck all over with three-cent postage-stamps. She took to decoration naturally; and so, you see, it is not entirely by choice that we are artists. We can not help it; the capacity and necessity are in men from the beginning. We have those very carved knife-handles to-day. They are rough things—only sharpened bits of flint—but there is no mistaking the art or the subject. And thus the so-called Decorative Art—art created to fill a particular place before decided on—is the most natural of all; for what is more natural than that men should adorn their dishes and weapons long before they create works to be simply hung upon walls to be admired? For a good while, in modern times, we most foolishly reversed all this: a handsome thing was made expressly to be handsome, and then was stuck up somewhere as an ornament. But within the last twenty years we are getting back to the right thing again; and it is surprising to see how soon a man learns to enjoy his coffee more out of a cup with a good and graceful shape than out of a clumsy and ugly one."

It is this decorative quality which modern art demands with increasing force, and without which it refuses to admit a painting into the category of approved work. In improving his opportunity to emphasize the fact, Mr. Blashfield has placed himself *en rapport* with the ruling contemporaneous spirit, and the interesting extract which we have quoted from his address before the Gotham students is significant as a sign of the times. That the pictures reproduced for this portfolio should reveal the operation of the same spirit is a matter of course, for they represent exclusively the present pictorial epoch, both in mode and in measure. Nor is it too much to say that, when an American artist of to-day begins to show a marked improvement in his work, when his paintings are talked of as promising, and public attention is directed to him as a man of the future, the usual cause of the success is a departure on his part in the direction of the deco-

rative, as Mr. Blashfield explains it. Of this truth no better illustration could be adduced than the "Breezy Day" of Mr. Charles C. Curran, and the "Expecta-

MARCUS SIMONS : *Richelieu at the Battle.*

tion" of Mr. Walter Blackman. Both these artists have made notable progress of late, and in the direction of what is decorative; and no sooner has this tendency been made manifest than it has attracted the attention of their fellow-artists and

48   RECENT IDEALS OF AMERICAN ART

the recognition of the intelligent public. And what more is meant by this choice and arrangement of the whole, which produces the decorative result, than the effort fully to express the sentiment of the beautiful? Or what more striking example of it than Mr. Marcius-Simons's "Richelieu at the Bastile," and "Pride and Pleasure"?

In Mr Inness's landscape "Peace and Plenty" we see the farthest advance that American art has yet made in the direction of the decorative, and, besides, the surest success in lifting the subject into the realms of poetry and imagination. To define precisely what is meant by these often-used and badly-abused terms would not be easy, nor is it needful. Let us say, simply, that the artist who succeeds in lifting his subject into the realms of poetry and imagination is at least one who has studied the processes of his art at their purest and rarest sources. Such an artist is Mr. George Inness. Some years ago it was my good fortune to have several conversations with this distinguished painter, which, with his permission, I preserved, in part, in the form of a magazine article, and I know of no better method of depicting these pure and rare sources, at which he has studied the processes of his art, than by quoting some of his own words. Had so thoughtful and capable a master as the late M. Eugène Fromentin been acquainted with the characteristic landscapes of Mr. Inness, it is not likely that he would have committed himself to the opinion, expressed in a letter from Brussels to a friend, that "Ruysdael is the first landscape-painter of the world—the equal, and perhaps the superior, of Claude Lorraine." Said Mr. Inness: "A work of art does not appeal to the intellect. It does not appeal to the moral sense. Its aim is not to instruct, not to edify, but to awaken an emotion. This emotion may be one of love, of pity, of veneration, of hate, of pleasure, or of pain; but it must be a single emotion, if the work have unity—as every such work should have—and the true beauty of the work consists in the beauty of the sentiment or emotion which it inspires. Its real greatness consists in the quality and force of the emotion. Details in the picture must be elaborated only enough fully to reproduce the impression that the artist wishes to reproduce. The effort and the difficulty of the artist are to make the thought clear and to preserve the unity of impression. If a painter could unite Meissonier's careful reproduction of details with Corot's inspirational power, he would be the very god of art. The reality of every artistic vision lies in the thought animating the artist's mind. This is proved by the fact that every artist who attempts only to imitate what he sees fails to represent that something which comes home to him as a satisfaction— fails to make a representation corresponding in the satisfaction which it produces

to the satisfaction felt in his first perception." Where in all the literature of art-criticism is there a sentence more expressive than this—"to represent that something which comes home to him as a satisfaction"?

In Mr. Thomas Hovenden's "Puzzled," an artisan sitting in his shop, we have a minor work of a painter who since the exhibition of his "Vendean Volunteer," at the Paris Exposition of 1878, has made rapid journeys along the route of his profession. Born in Ireland in 1840, educated in the atelier of Cabanel, and at the National Academy in New York, and at present a resident

GEORGE INNESS : *Peace and Plenty.*

of a suburb of Philadelphia, Mr. Hovenden is in no sense provincial. He paints with a careful brush the products of a painstaking mind. He is sure of himself as far as he goes; for, before starting, he understands precisely whither and for what he is to go. Not long since an artist of some distinction in Paris painted a picture which he called "The Widow." It represented a French lady, in mourning robes, just leaving the cemetery where her husband was buried. To a spectator who thought of buying the picture, but who objected that its sentiment was too sad, the painter responded: "I'll tell you what I can do. In France, the costume worn by widows resembles that worn by women who go to be churched, except that the color is black instead of purple. Now, if the picture in its present condition is too gloomy a one, I will wipe out the cemetery, and change the robe from black to purple; then, instead of a widow, you will have a woman who has just been churched." Mr. Hovenden's conceptions, being not so facile, are not so readily transformed.

The author of the "Route de Concarneau," Mr. W. L. Picknell, an effect of intense sunshine on a sandy road, now owned by Mr. Thomas B. Clarke, has been for some years a student of the picturesque fishermen and fisherwomen of the extreme western coast of Brittany, where the sketch for "Waiting for a Bite" also was made. Like several other American artists, notably Mr. Henry Mosler and Mr. Alexander Harrison, this painter has a real affection for the almost primeval simplicity of life in Finistère, or the Land's End of France, where the peasantry have no ambition whatever to be considered like the Parisians, where the tide of foreign travel never flows, and where the souls and the costumes are to the manner born. When the Europeans entered Japan, the art of that country became so transformed that it may almost be said to have vanished. Its individuality disappeared. The inroads of the foreigners have deprived many districts in France of that picturesqueness which artists admired in the peasantry. But along the extreme western shores, especially at Concarneau and Pont-Aven, some American artists have found a page of Nature pure and simple, and it is not to be wondered that they read it with delight. Mr. Picknell does not paint models, as is the manner of many of his countrymen. He paints the living men and women of every-day life, in their own clothes, and with their characteristic expressions; and he is a master of movement and of the dramatic.

We again encounter Mr. Charles Sprague Pearce, with his fine facility, and his gracious and elevated style, in "Across the Fields," and "St. Geneviève." Often as the last-named subject has been treated in pictorial art, and even in view of those superb mural decorations in the Pantheon of Paris, by M. Puvis de Chevannes, it is but just to say that Mr. Pearce's interesting performance is its own raison d'être. This charming figure of the legendary lore of France—the patron saint of Paris, who in her childhood was the object of the admiration of her neighbors for her piety and for the sweetness of her disposition, who frequently was seen praying in the fields where she tended her father's sheep, and for whom an illustrious archbishop predicted a great career—has presented itself to Mr. Pearce's imagination with freshness and distinctness, and he has painted her in the same spirit in which the late M. Bastien-Lepage painted his celebrated "Joan of Arc."

The ability to express a dramatic subject is as rare in the studio as on the
stage, and the difficulty of painting the "Mystery" of Mr. Carl Marr, considered
simply as a piece of technique, is extraordinary. Landscape, sea-scape, and the
nude, made their demands upon him, and it is only just to say that he has

THOMAS HOVENDEN : *Puzzled.*

responded to them with success. Hanging in an excellent position on the line,
in one of the well-lighted galleries of the Metropolitan Museum of Art, this
interesting picture attracts the notice of the amateur and the unlearned alike,
while the professional artist who stands before it admires the skill in which it
abounds. No spectator endowed with a heart can fail to be touched by the

tragedy which it depicts. An aged wanderer—perhaps the "Wandering Jew" of the legend—encounters on the sea-shore the dead body of a beautiful young woman, and his thoughts are directed afresh to the mystery of life. If she was to be thus untimely cut off, why was she brought into existence at all? What is her name, her station, her story? Has she a father or mother, a brother or sister? Did she seek death, or did death seek her? Was her gift of beauty a fatal gift, and does her pitiless fate express once again man's inhumanity to woman? If anybody was to be taken, why not the tottering old outcast who meditates upon the untowardness of her destiny? It is all a mystery, and the painter leaves it where life leaves it, unexplained but pathetic in the extreme, and full of poetry in its deep-blue sky and watching stars and surging sea, its loneliness and desolation, its contrast between living and dead, between youth and age, between beauty and the wreck of wasting years. There is no indecision in the artist's touch, and no embarrassment in his purpose. With the resources of a technical education in Europe, and the poetry of a grand conception, he has bent himself to the accomplishment of his task, and has acquitted himself with distinction. Especially has the nude—always difficult of expression, not only in itself, but because it must be consulted in the cold light of the studio, and under conditions almost sure to produce conventionalism, in pose at least—been treated by Mr. Marr in the spirit of a young master. The Metropolitan Museum of Art may be congratulated upon the possession of this picture, which it owes to the generosity of Mr. George I. Seney, of New York city. Nor is this his only gift. At least fifteen other oil-paintings in the collection came from the same source.

Mr. W. H. Lippincott, like most of the Americans whose works are reproduced in this portfolio, has recently pursued a systematic course of study in Europe, and, if his style of painting betrays no suggestion of his master, M. Bonnat, this is no more than might have been expected. His sympathies seem to be rather with the Ecouen school of the late Edouard Frère, but his touch is more vigorous, and his sense of color more acute. His children are prettier than those of Frère, and most of them are in more prosperous circumstances. After painting some charming Brittany specimens at Pont-Aven in Finistère, Lippincott returned to America and opened a studio in New York, although Philadelphia had the first claim upon him, being the city of his birth. He soon became a professor in the schools of the National Academy of Design, where his canvases had already been honorably hung. At the monthly exhibitions of the Union League Club, and at the annual displays of the Society of American Artists, he was warmly greeted in the best of company. His "Harmony" may be considered as the most

representative of his works. It belongs to the collection of Mr. Washington Wilson, and the child who plays at the piano is an excellent type of the younger set in Mr. Ward McAllister's famous " Four Hundred."

The " Grand Time" of Mr. W. P. W. Dana, sometimes exhibited under the title of " Stormy Weather," depicts a French fisherman in his boat shortening sail -not because he has mortal fears of the situation, but because by this means he

WILLIAM L. PICKNELL : *Waiting for a Bite*.

can enjoy it better. A thorough old salt like himself is rather stimulated than otherwise by the bad weather, and has a better time than when lazily drifting like the " Lotos-Eaters." In earlier years Mr. Dana used to be fond of painting historical marines, like the " Chase of the Frigate Constitution," in Mr. William Astor's collection ; but his more recent tastes incline him to subjects less pretentious— the breakers and the seaweed-gatherers of the Brittany coast. The ocean has the same charms for him that it had for Byron, and all his pictures show a deep affection. For many years he has enjoyed the reputation of being the most accomplished

American marine painter in France. Frenchmen sometimes smile at Mr. Whistler's representing the United States, after spending his life in Paris and in London; but Mr. Dana did return to America after ten years at the École des Beaux-Arts and in the Parisian suburbs, and became a National Academician and an intimate of our leading collectors. He passed the summer of 1888 in the north of Scotland, and has for many years made his home in France. Dana's waves look like waves, and his seas abound in the romance of the seas. He is both poet and painter.

Mr. Francis D. Millet's easiest success has been with *genre* subjects like "The Cozy Corner," "The Click of the Latch," and "The Window-Seat," where a sweet-faced country girl is occupying herself indoors; but he has painted portraits also, and of late has rivaled Alma-Tadema himself in themes like the Pompeiian "Water-Carrier," which we have reproduced from Mr. George I. Seney's collection. Mr. Millet, besides being a painter, has won distinction as a "war correspondent" and a contributor to the literary magazines. He is most painstaking in his methods, and has for years been a warm personal friend of Alma-Tadema, which may explain in part the direction of his later work. Among his best-known portraits are those of Lawrence Barrett and Samuel L. Clemens. The "Landscape and Sheep" of Mr. R. W. Van Boskerck bears the mark of a young and healthful talent nourished on the best traditions of art and inspired by the contemporaneous spirit. Mr. Van Boskerck is one of the few Americans whose works appear on exhibition from time to time in the Goupil Gallery in New York, and the picture by him which we have reproduced was hanging in that place a few months ago, whence it was removed for purposes of reproduction through the courtesy of Mr. Julius Oehme. No young American has shown greater advance in the direction followed by the colorist than Mr. Van Boskerck; he has surprised his friends and patrons by the promise of his work in this regard, and his latest pictures are in all respects his best. Nor is there another young American who depends less upon what are known as "sensational" subjects in landscape. A sunlight meadow, an old stone fence, and a grazing flock, are sufficient for his purpose, with little concern for the human element. He does not stop to ask himself whether or not the human element would add interest to his subject. It is enough that without it his subject is interesting to him; and he will make it so to others by his ingenuousness of purpose, his gift for artistic selection, and his easy and indicative drawing.

An agreeable painting, on the line, in the private collection of Mr. William T. Evans, of Van Vorst Square, Jersey City, is "The Diligence" of Mr. Wordsworth

Thompson, a transcript of an Italian scene, rich in picturesqueness and full of movement.   Mr. Thompson is one of our National Academicians who has felt the

Marcius-Simons : *Pride and Pleasure*

touch of the *Zeitgeist*, and his work belongs of right to this collection, which deals with the latest era of American art. Certain of his canvases exhibited recently in the rooms of the American Art Association and at the National Gallery are painted with even more breadth than this one, especially a New England farm-scene, and a Revolutionary sketch in which military officers appear near an inn by the wayside. In the study of historical themes this artist is indefatigable; but he treats modern subjects with equal success, and, indeed, has not been known as a painter of any special class of motives, though his preference has usually been for landscapes with small figures. He never uses hieroglyphic characters in expressing his sentiment; nor does he write a hand so obscure that only the initiated can appreciate him.

Few American paintings of recent date are better known than Mr. J. L. Stewart's "Hunt Ball," with its scarlet coats, its white gowns, and its prevailing tone of contemporaneous gayety. To the courtesy of Mr. George I. Seney we are indebted for permission to reproduce this striking picture, which was hung in the place of honor in the galleries of the Brooklyn Art Association on the occasion of Mr. Seney's exhibiting his collection of paintings for the benefit of a deserving charity. As the spectator entered the place, the first object to engage his attention was the "Hunt Ball," on the line, in the center of the southern wall; and the nearer he drew to it, the brighter it seemed. So popular was the work, that many persons were inclined to attribute to its presence alone much of the financial success of the exhibition; and even after the lapse of more than eighteen months its fine decorative quality is remembered in Brooklyn as the most salient feature of the display. Mr. Stewart has had unusual advantages in the pursuit of his profession. His father, long a resident of Paris, and the owner of one of its most valuable and, undoubtedly, its most interesting, private collection of art-works, said to the son, when the latter proposed to become a painter: "Well, my boy, follow out your inclination, but under one condition. I will have no trifling. If you are to be a painter, you must be a serious one. No half-way measures will do. You must give yourself entirely and unreservedly to the work. You must begin at the bottom and go step by step in the ascent, with nothing to divert or to satisfy until you have reached the summit." The condition was accepted by the ardent young painter, and the father proceeded to put at his command all needed opportunities for travel and study, for familiarizing one's self with the best that is or has been thought or known in the department of painting. In Spain the artist became the friend and admirer of the brilliant Fortuny, some of whose noblest works—especially the "Choice of a Model"—have since

become the property of Mr. Stewart the elder. The talents of Madrazo also interested him, and, needless to say, the triumphs of Velasquez's great genius, as seen in the galleries of Madrid and of Seville. To that singularly gifted painter, the lamented Baudry, whose brush has ennobled the ceiling of the Opera-House in Paris, the affection of the aspiring American was turned at an early period of his career, and nowhere in the world has the admirer of that master a better opportunity of studying the beauty of his easel-work than in the collection made

EDWIN L. WEEKS : *Arrival of Prince Humbert.*

by Mr. Stewart's father in the Avenue d'Iéna, Paris. Under the instruction of Madrazo, of Zamacois, and of Gérôme, Julius L. Stewart came into intimate relations with the modern spirit in portraiture and in historical *genre*. He is to-day one of the recognized masters in portrait-painting—a master who sees into the spiritual possibilities of his sitters, and who can portray those possibilities under pictorial conditions. If occasionally he lays himself open to the charge of flattering some of his fashionable patrons, the same can be said of most successful portraitists, who seem to follow the counsel given by Fitz-Greene Halleck to Thomas Hicks:

"I want you to paint me so that I shall look like a gentleman. Never mind the likeness. In fifty years nobody will be able to tell whether the portrait is a likeness or not; but I want to be handed down to posterity as a gentleman." Nor would Mr. Stewart be apt to turn a deaf ear to a sitter who should say to him, as was once said to a well-known Paris painter by a lady who had come to his studio: "I wish you, Mr. Artist, to give me a chin; I haven't any of my own. My forehead is pretty and my eyes are divine, but Nature forgot to add to them a chin." "Certainly, madame," was the reply, "you shall have a chin, by all means." One of the best-known portraits of an American by M. Carolus Duran is that of a lady whose natural height is about five feet three inches. On canvas she presents a graceful and imposing figure, at least six inches taller. Her grandchildren, she says, will have no cause to regret the painter's course. But Mr. Stewart is a truth-seeker all the same; he paints character, and he paints it with the decorative quality. A recent example of his work is the portrait of Mme. Rothschild in a gown of yellow silk. He is now painting a companion-picture to the "Hunt Ball," entitled the "Supper after the Ball," which shows a series of figures similarly clothed, some of the women holding in their hands the favors received during the cotillion—a work which, like its predecessor in this portfolio, abounds in grace of movement, in facial animation and variety, and in the subtlest apprehension of the festal spirit. Mr. Stewart's studio, it may be added, is one of the largest and best-equipped in Paris. Several unfinished canvases are always to be found upon his easels, but buyers are too eager for the finished ones to allow them to remain long. It will be twenty years, perhaps, before this artist may be said to have reached his prime. His success is already extraordinary, and, as his industry keeps pace with it (and his ambition is boundless), the future promises much. His principal contributions to the *Salon* have been as follows: In 1878, "La Maja" and "La Lecture"; in 1879, "Portrait de Lady A——"; in 1882, "Portrait de Mlle. E. S." and "L'Été"; in 1883, "Portrait de Mme. ——" and "Une Cour au Caire, Égypte"; in 1884, "A Five-o'clock Tea," the picture which first made him widely known, the subject being some fashionable men and women drinking tea on a veranda; in 1885, the "Hunt Ball." His reputation is a celebrity rather than a mere notoriety, and it has come to him at a period when, at least across the Atlantic, the successful artist is a social prince, a reigning favorite.

The Goupil Gallery, in the Avenue de l'Opéra, Paris, contained in the summer of 1887 an oil-painting, the "Shepherd and his Flock," by a young American, Mr. G. S. Truesdell, almost unknown to his countrymen, but which had been

purchased by Messrs. Goupil & Co., because of its merits, and been placed on
exhibition by them in one of those windows looking out toward the Opera-House
that are the cynosure of visitors and the desire of painters.   No American artist
ever forgot the impression made
upon him by the sight of his first
picture in the window of the Goupil
establishment.   Through the kindness of the Messrs. Goupil, and the
courtesy of Mr. Truesdell, the canvas was taken from its frame and
sent to the photographic studio at
Asnières, near Paris, where a negative was made from it for the
purpose of obtaining the beautiful
photogravure that appears in this
collection.   Mr. Truesdell is neither
revolutionary nor sensational in his
methods.   On the contrary, he has
simplicity and directness, and he
chooses his subjects, not because of
their easiness, but rather because of
the number of pictorial problems
that they involve.   Here we have
figure-painting, animal-painting and
landscape-painting combined.   The

CHARLES SPRAGUE PEARCE : *Across the Fields.*

drawing is facile and sure, the touch is broad, the generalization perfect, the
ensemble artistic.   The sturdy, honest shepherd leads his sheep, as in contemporaneous France and ancient Judea, not drives them, as in the United States of
America; and his face betrays a feeling almost paternal.   There is a religious
element in this picture, and Mr. Truesdell might have intended to illustrate that
fine old Hebrew verse, "He shall lead his flock like a shepherd," although it is
more likely that his purpose was merely to paint the fact as he had seen and
studied it in the smiling fields of Normandy.   His canvas is one that makes the
intelligent spectator reason and think.

    Mr. Ernest Parton has achieved recognition from the fact that the British
Government recently bought one of his landscapes, and his prosperity certainly
began with his resolution to paint in England rather than in America.   Some of

the best examples of his work are in the possession of Dr. William Carr, of New York city, who has allowed the "Pond Lilies" to be reproduced for this book. A profound feeling for sunshine and for atmosphere pervades Mr. Parton's work, which appeals to no special tastes, but pleases all wholesome tastes. In "Pride and Pleasure"—the pleasure of the young father and the pride of the young mother— Mr. Marcius-Simons touches the popular heart and attracts the cultivated sense. The "Arrival of Prince Humbert," by Mr. E. L. Weeks, is a characteristic study of East Indian architecture and the regal life of Asia. The "Lady of Shalott," which adorns the cover of the portfolio, is Mrs. Odenheimer Fowler's delightful conception of Tennyson's well-known heroine.

CHARLES SPRAGUE PEARCE : *St. Geneviève.*

IV.

CHARLES X. HARRIS : *The Watchmaker.*

EXPLAIN it as we may, the fact remains that the annals of our civil war have not been recorded by our painters. The United States have produced neither a De Neuville nor a Detaille, nor even a feeble imitator of those successful artists. Only occasionally do we find an American offering to his country a pictorial souvenir of the greatest and most memorable conflict that ever engaged the labors and fixed the destinies of a nation. Though it is now nearly twenty-five years since the war ended, no painter has appeared either as the historian of the struggle or the recorder of its leading and most characteristic incidents. Several of our best-known artists were soldiers in the army, brave and patriotic; and one of them, Mr. F. S. Church, has declared that it was only the humors of the war that appealed to his pencil; that he never felt in the least inclined to make sketches of its serious aspects. Mr. Winslow Homer, to be sure, has painted several scenes in the struggle, and has contributed to the illustrated periodicals many sketches in black-and-white; the late Mr. Sanford R. Gifford, a member of the Seventh Regiment of New York, has left one or two reminiscences in oils; Mr. Gilbert Gaul, though too young to have been a participant in the strife, has, nevertheless, produced some excellent battle-scenes; and Mr. W. H. Shelton, in "A Recollection of Gettysburg," which appears in this portfolio, has depicted an incident which his own eyes saw, and of which he was a principal part. We are indebted to him also for a very interesting verbal description of the scene, which, of itself, is a valuable contribution to the annals of the civil war. Mr. Shelton writes: "The line of Federal artillery, which extended from Round Top on the left to and along Cemetery Heights, made a sharp turn outside the cemetery-gate. One battery covered the approach by the road from the village, and three others on its right were planted to meet a flank attack from that direction. Reynolds's battery was at the extreme right. One of its guns had been lost on the first day, during the running fight through the village, which ended in the concentration of the First and Eleventh Corps on Cemetery Hill. Four of the remaining guns were planted in a stubble-field across the Baltimore pike; and the sixth, which was my command, held position below the wall and in the next field. During the evening of the 2d of July, 1863, we had repulsed a vigorous night-attack of infantry from the direction of the village, which sought to envelop that flank.

"All the morning of the 3d, however, we had been undisturbed, listening to occasional infantry-firing, which seemed at times to almost surround us in horse-shoe shape, with the open side toward Baltimore. At about twelve o'clock an ominous silence rested over both armies. The cannoneers and drivers of the gun below the wall were lounging against that structure but a few paces from the parallel line of artillerymen. I had thrown the reins of my saddle-horse over the handles of the limber, and had seated myself on the turf near the wall. Suddenly, a mile away to our front, a puff of white smoke shot out from the hill-side. We knew it was a shell coming our way, but not a man of us thought it worth while to get on his feet because of a single shell. In a moment, however, the shrieking missile, cleaving and burning the air in its flight, swept so low that it seemed to come between the line of men and the line of horses. An express train, tearing along beside them, would not have been so terrifying to the animals, nor have so completely separated them from the men. When a screaming shell passes so near a man that he can not tell whether it sounds the louder in his right ear or in his left, even the most experienced soldier thinks for an instant that his time has come. The whistling retreat of the missile in the distance is the sweetest sound he ever heard.

JAMES M. HART   *Under the Trees*

"While the artillerymen crowded against the wall, the horses swerved to the right, and in their terror plunged down the hill, the leaders falling and the others rolling headlong over them, in a hopeless tangle of beasts, harness, and wheels. We addressed ourselves at once to the business of disentanglement, and our invisible enemy directed his fire at the living mass. One of his shells struck a stone wall fifty yards away and directly in line for us, sending up a cloud of dust and stones. In the most favorable circumstances, the patience requisite to extricate a number of plunging horses from such a tangle of wheels and harness would have been exemplary. But we were under fire all the time. Still, our problem was successfully solved, and the runaway limber was returned to its place beside the wall. Meantime, General Lee's artillery, in advance of Pickett's celebrated charge, had opened fire on the Union lines along the Cemetery Ridge; while, on our side, miles of guns, ranged as closely as they could conveniently be served, were sharing in the fiercest artillery duel of the war. In an incredibly short space of time the clouds of smoke had made the mid-afternoon of that July day as dark as twilight. Added to the roar of the guns were the humming and hissing of innumerable fragments of exploded shells. Protected by the hill, and partly behind the line in action, we had leisure to observe the fearful scene. In the cemetery, behind the old brick gateway, men and horses, evergreens and monuments, were as gray as effects in a thick fog. I remember distinctly to have seen a black horse, stripped of his harness, walking between the rows of gravestones, dragging his entrails on the ground, and tossing his head up and down as I have often seen a horse in a pasture when a vicious fly was stinging him under the jowl." Mr. Shelton has painted his recollection of Gettysburg with feeling and with skill.

Another battle-scene, painted also with feeling and skill, is Mr. Julian O. Davidson's remarkable picture of Commodore De Kay taking the Cacique. In this instance the artist had the advantage of being inspired by one of the most romantic and brilliant engagements in the annals of naval warfare. George Coleman De Kay, a descendant of Guillaume de Key, of Haarlem, one of the earliest settlers on Manhattan Island, was as gallant an officer and as brave a seaman as this country has produced. When a mere lad he ran away from school and entered the merchant service. During the war between Brazil and the Argentine Republic, in 1827, he was offered a captaincy in the navy of the latter country; but, preferring to earn his rank rather than to accept it as a gift, he left Buenos Ayres in the small brig General Brandzen, and soon captured, in successive engagements, the Brazilian schooner-of-war Isabella, with five guns and forty-one men, the Brazilian brigs Flor de Verdad, with twelve guns, and Princesa, with fourteen guns, and several merchantmen; besides giving sixty slaves their freedom. Not relishing the situation in the least, the Brazilian Government dispatched one of its bravest and most trusted officers, Captain George Manson, in

his fine brig-of-war, the Cacique, with instructions to seize the General Brandzen and bring her into Rio. George De Kay was not yet twenty-five years old, but on that day he won the rank of commodore for the magnificent victory which Mr. Davidson's brush has depicted.

It was three o'clock on Sunday afternoon when the Cacique, with fourteen guns and one hundred and twenty-two men, overhauled the General Brandzen, with eight guns and forty-one men, off the coast of Pernambuco, the inhabitants

F. S. CHURCH : *Peace.*

of which thronged the hills to see the capture of De Kay and his pernicious little privateer. But they were disappointed. After a severe engagement, De Kay succeeded in boarding the Cacique, although all his officers and many of his best men were wounded. Captain Manson offered him his sword, which the victor would not accept, owing to the personal bravery which his adversary had shown. From the nature of the wounds which De Kay himself had received, he could scarcely muster strength to crawl down into the cabin. The Cacique had lost eighteen killed, the General Brandzen only one. In 1847 the distinguished commodore projected and executed the scheme of carrying provisions to starving Ireland in

United States men-of-war. The story of his life is a stirring epic, and the name of De Kay is a treasure to his country. Mr. Davidson has deservedly received many words of appreciation for the beauty of his wave-drawing, and the fidelity with which he has conceived the spirit of the action; and he can afford to rest his reputation upon this meritorious work. He has painted other naval battles than this, and Mr. Shelton has painted other war-pictures than the "Recollection of Gettysburg"; and these two artists, with Mr. Gilbert Gaul, whose work in a similar direction may be reproduced in a future number of this portfolio, are the leading battle-painters of the present epoch.

As long ago as 1855 an English critic of reputation (Mr. William Michael Rossetti) recorded that the dominant impulse in art, at that time, was toward realism, and by realism he meant a conception of things in their actual and essential character, and an endeavor to convey this conception by a serious adhesion to facts. Even so noticeable a classicist as Ingres, he observed, was no exception to the rule; his small pictures, then hanging at the Paris International Exposition, were concerned with history or historic anecdote, and even in his idealism the element of realism could be discerned. Delacroix and Delaroche were moving in the realistic direction as truly as Millais and Holman Hunt, though under divergent aspects; and great was the number of French paintings that reproduced the true life and occupations of the people in a positive and trenchant spirit. Even in the German school the stronger men were grafting realism upon "the theoretic or abstract stock which they cultivated." The realistic tendency, indeed, "seemed to some extent to be connected with the modern love of landscape"; and from natural truth in landscape proper the step was easy to the same truth in backgrounds of figure-subjects; and, this result being reached, it would scarcely do to allow the figures themselves to contradict the actuality of the impression as a whole. Upon this last suggestion, however, our English critic "would not venture to lay any particular stress." Thirty-three years have elapsed since these words were written, and it excites a smile to learn that a modern art-critic should have needed to insist that, with natural truth in landscape and natural truth in the backgrounds of figure-subjects, natural truth was proper also in the figures themselves. Certainly, the contemporaneous pictures reproduced in this portfolio discover on the part of the artists a decided sympathy with "the true life and occupations of the people." Mr. F. C. Jones shows it; Mr. Percy Moran, Mr. Millet, and Mr. McEwen show it. Mr. Brush has gone to Canada and the Western wilds to inform himself concerning the habits and social customs of the Indians. Mr. Harris studies a watchmaker with the assiduity that a watchmaker studies a watch.

Mr. Keller engages his attention with the bright faces of successful fisher-lads and their youthful companions. Mr. Lippincott studies harmony in a little child at a piano, and little kittens supping on the floor. And if Mr. Blashfield diverges into a grand allegorical composition, and acquaints us with the doings of the Muses, or if Mr. Maynard impersonates the genius of Civilization, we feel that the case

H. WOLCOTT ROBBINS : *A Mountain Road.*

is exceptional, and that even an artist must have his occasional "night off"; while to suggest that the realistic tendency "may possibly be to some extent connected with the modern love of landscape" is not at all likely to startle the admirers of Mr. G. H. Smillie's idyl "In Connecticut," or Mr. Ogden Wood's pastoral "In the Open."

While the realism of Mr. F. C. Jones's "Don't Cry" may strike many persons as akin to that of the founder of the Ecouen school, M. Edouard Frère, there is a frankness, a directness, a simplicity in the work of the American which his French predecessor does not exhibit. M. Frère's pictures lack the *naïveté* and spontaneity of Mr. Jones's most characteristic examples, and their sentiment verges closer upon sentimentality. One feels that the staying quality of the Frenchman's talents is inferior to that of the American's, and this because it is truth that lasts, rather than the semblance of truth. And if we accept a French definition of the word picturesque, and understand by it the sentiment of life in its most familiar form, Mr. Jones's vital and ingenuous *genres* must be regarded as picturesque in the most obvious sense. They convey the charm of a scene in common life by producing the illusion of reality, and of them may be said what the same French critic has said of Charles Jacque's most successful subjects—his truant children roaming about the fields, his ducks in a mill-pond, his village streets, and his old barns—that, without recourse to any tricks, they show us, in plastic language, familiar things or persons as these are in nature. "Charles Jacque saw, one day, a broken old wheelbarrow with the aspect, and particularly the color, bestowed on rural implements by long use. He offered the owner a new one in exchange for the old, and the bargain was soon settled, to the satisfaction of both parties. There are few collectors of prints who do not now possess the picture of this old wheelbarrow. It is in a corner of one of his compositions, near a manure-heap, where hens are pecking. On a neighboring farm there was an old shepherd-dog, long past all service, whose name was Capitaine. Charles Jacque thought the dog superb, and, intending to introduce him in his pictures, bought him, to the amazement of the shepherd and of the farmers, who discussed among themselves the motive that might have led to the purchase of the animal." They at last came to the conclusion that "the gentleman from Paris" was making a collection of old and infirm brutes, and in a short time he found himself in a position to buy with the utmost ease a wonderful array of mangy dogs, lame chickens, and afflicted sheep. The original of Mr. Jones's picture is in the collection of Mr. Benjamin Altman.

In "The Old Song," owned by Mr. Thomas B. Clarke, we meet again that sympathetic artist and accomplished painter, Mr. Percy Moran, whose canvas representing three young women gossiping over their tea, was reproduced in an earlier part of this portfolio. Mr. Moran has made his reputation, not by novelty of methods nor by oddity of subjects, but by intelligent painstaking. He is as little inclined to "dash off" his compositions as is Alma-Tadema, and he does not send to the exhibitions mere "effects of color" in sumptuous frames. An inspection of "The

GEORGE D. BRUSH : *Mourning her Brave.*

Old Song" made by the penetrative and relentless camera, which often sees much
more in a canvas than does the human eye, would show that the dress of the high-
bred woman who sits improvising at the piano is by no means the result of a single
painting. Mr. Moran tried more than once, before obtaining what he sought.

Mr. George H. Boughton, a native of England, and long a resident of the United States, has for many years made his home in London, although not relinquishing his American citizenship. He has been a member of the National Academy of Design since 1871, and an Associate of the London Royal Academy since 1879, and whenever a vacancy occurs in the list of members of the latter institution his name is sure to be mentioned in connection with proposals to supply it. He is a graduate of no art-school, either in this country or in Europe, but has made himself one of the most accomplished and successful of living painters. His beautiful house in London, where so many Americans have been entertained, was built out of the proceeds of his well-directed toil, and the compositions which he paints bear the unquestioned stamp of originality. A recent exhibition at Avery's art-rooms in New York city, of his collected works, mostly lent by American and English owners, was one of the notable events of the season. Mr. Boughton uses his pen as well as his pencil, and has contributed to the leading magazines some interesting descriptions of rambles in Holland and elsewhere, with illustrations by himself. He is best known by his interpretations of Puritan life—maidens in the fields or on the sea-shore, and soldiers, like Miles Standish—but the range of his brush is wide. He has depicted the duel from "Twelfth Night," the issuing of William the Testy's edict against tobacco-smoking, the Dismal Swamp, Venus and Adonis, Milton visited by Andrew Marvel, the Burgomaster's daughter, the Normandy girl, and the winter landscapes of Northern New York. Among his single figures "The Page," owned by Mr. Thomas B. Clarke, is an excellent example. It challenges thought in the beholder.

Of Mr. F. S. Church it is sometimes said that he possesses fancy rather than imagination, but, as Mr. Ruskin, in the preface to his rearranged edition of "Modern Painters," confesses that he no longer cares for such distinctions, and that he is now entirely indifferent which word he uses, Mr. Church's critics can settle the matter among themselves. "I should say of a work of art," continues Mr. Ruskin, "that it was 'fancied' or well 'invented,' or well 'imagined,' with only some shades of different meaning in the application of the terms, rather dependent on the matter treated than the power of mind involved in the treatment. I might agree with Sir Piercie Shafton that his doublet was well fancied, or that his figure of speech was well conceived, and might, perhaps, reserve the word 'imagination' for the design of an angel's dress by Giotto, or the choice of a simile by Dante. But such distinctions are scarcely more than varieties of courtesy or dignity in the use of words; and I could not in essential nature of faculty distinguish Sir Piercie's designing from Giotto's, except, as I have said,

with respect to the matter of it, and the fixture of his attention rather on the dress than the angel. Briefly, the power of the human mind to invent circumstances, forms, or scenes, at its pleasure, may be generally and properly called 'imagination.'" Accordingly, this writer, who once did so much to establish distinctions between "fancy" and "imagination," solemnly warns his readers not to trouble themselves with them. Mr. Church's friends have always conceded to him the possession of fancy, and now they may claim excellent authority, if they

ARTHUR I. KELLER : "See him Squirm."

choose, for insisting that the author of such a picture as "Peace" has been endowed with imagination also. Mr. Church has done more than any other American toward the establishment of a truly national school of American art, and, as I have recently expressed myself at some length in *Harper's Magazine* concerning his work, as a whole, I may, perhaps, be permitted to quote here a few words from that article: "Mr. Church's distinction as a painter consists in having created, in a series of idyls, the most beautiful woman in American art. She may be called our first American woman, very much in the sense that Mr. Lowell has called Abraham Lincoln our first American man. She never was incarnated until Mr. Church incarnated her. She is a personage as distinct as she is vital and satisfying. She has all the poetry of lines and color in dress, all the seductive undulation of robes, that characterizes the Tanagra figurines. She is clothed in drapery rather than in gowns. She feels, as did Eugénie de Guerin, that it does her good to be going about in the midst of our enchanting nature, with blossoms, birds, and verdure all around her, under the large and blue sky; but, unlike Eugénie, she never experiences the *ennui* that finds at the bottom of everything only emptiness and nothingness. In her ingenuousness she reminds one of the young singing girls of Luca della Robbia, while, at the same time, she stands forth as an image of the intellectual movement that governs the age to which she belongs. Being our first American woman, we respect her as a unique and lovable type in a civilization where the emotions have become less simple as the heart has become more skeptical. At ten years of age Mr. Church painted, in crude water-colors on sheets of foolscap paper, a wondrous panorama of Indians, pirates, and highwaymen performing most blood-thirsty deeds. At thirteen he left his home in Grand Rapids, Michigan, to work for the American Express Company in Chicago, where he was known among his comrades as 'the artistic chap,' because he had a talent for drawing comic sketches with the pencil. At seventeen he entered the Federal army as a private, and served as such for three years, until the close of the War for the Union. One of his messmates speaks of him as a notable shot with the cannon and a brave soldier, but he never had any impulse to paint battles, and his country lost a possible De Neuville. What struck his imagination most in that awful and prolonged contest was the comic side of tenting on the old camp-ground. At twenty-six, after renewing his service with the American Express Company, he worked as a draughtsman for a wood-engraver of machinery, and was considered the worst draughtsman his employer had. Walter Shirlaw, then teaching art in the Academy in Chicago, first started the amateurist young draughtsman on a serious road by introducing him to the opportunities of the life-school of that institution; and Professor Wilmarth, of the National Academy of Design in New York—whither he had removed—followed up the advantages of such a course, while the artist supported himself by making comic sketches. Nevertheless, it is evident that nothing just related explains the conditions that produced our first American woman—the woman who appears in "Peace" and scores of other compositions. A brave soldier for more than three years, a business man, a comic

W. H. Lippincott *Child et*

illustrator, what was there in the influence of his *milieu* to bring into existence
so delightful an ideal? Why did he not paint the battle-scenes *quorum magna*

pars fuit? Why did he prefer the comic to the serious? And how was it that when, at last, his comic sketches did not sell, he turned his attention to our first American woman, with such success that he himself, by this time, must be tired of his old flame, Miss Amanda Jenkins, of Podunk, who, while visting the Aquarium, sits down on the African tortoise, thinking it a stool, her new red rose meanwhile being stolen from her bonnet by the voracious giraffe? In several of his pictures he had the co-operation as sitter of an interesting girl of twelve years, who was introduced to his notice by the fact that her mother once sent her on an errand to his studio while she was on her way to school. Perhaps, on one eventful afternoon, he saw her face in contrast with some bear-skin or tiger-skin hanging upon the walls of the room, and a glimmer of the subject that has since enthralled his pencil may have stolen across his imagination. For years he has been a student of wild animals in the Central Park; and one memorable day, when the action of a caged tiger was interesting him, he might have seen a fair young American also watching the same wild beast, and the contrast between a beautiful girl and a magnificent animal might have begun to attract him. Certainly, all his subjects and all his values are based on nature, fantastic though many of them seem"; and certainly, also, he has never set foot upon the soil of Europe, but has done all his studying in the United States.

In common with many other young painters represented in this collection, Mr. Church labors under the disadvantage—or, shall we say, advantage—of appearing in his first manner. His work is tentative as yet, and so is the work of Mr. C. X. Harris (whose "Watchmaker" serves the purpose of a *lettre ornée*), Mr. W. J. Whittemore, with his mermaid on the rocks, Mr. W. H. Lippincott, Mr. G. D. Brush, Mr. Carleton Wiggins, Mr. Ogden Wood, and many others. No one can be sure that these artists are destined to improve upon their first manner; nor, on the other hand, can he be sure that they are not so destined. Their present efforts represent them in their present *milieu* and with their present equipment. Their last pictures may be their best, as was the case with Raphael; or, their last pictures may be their worst, as was the case with William Page. But, in any event, these men are worth listening to, because, in most instances, they are really representing themselves, and not other artists, American or foreign. In their "first manner" they are spontaneous and individual. You do not feel the presence of their teachers. And of no other young painters in the civilized world is this statement so generally and so often true. The conventional studio statistics, which always set forth the name of the master under whom an artist has studied, are less significant in the case of young Americans of the present

epoch than in the
case of any other
young artists of any
epoch; and the rea-
son is that, with
their realistic aims
and ambitions, each
tries to see Nature
with his own eyes,
and to reproduce
the impression that
Nature makes upon
him without regard
to the formulas of
the Academy or the

CHARLES SPRAGUE PEARCE : *Gathering Herbs.*

particular methods of the academic teachers.   How many pupils, for instance,
after learning the rudiments of art in the atelier of M. Gérôme at the École des

CARLETON WIGGINS : *Evening in the Village of Gres, France.*

Beaux-Arts, have proceeded to paint pictures which, in subject and in manner, bear not the faintest resemblance to the masterpieces of that distinguished Frenchman? This fact, indeed, is one that most frequently and forcibly strikes the reader of the annual *Salon* catalogue, in which, to the name of each artist-exhibitor, there is attached the name of the master under whom he studied. Sometimes two, and occasionally even three, masters are enumerated as the teachers of the same painter; and it is both pleasing and instructive to note how diverse in purpose and in practice these teachers usually are. When Raphael's early works are examined, we feel the influence of his master, Perugino; and it is only in the pictures of his last period that we are able to perceive evidences of his release— a release often effected, to be sure, at the expense of simplicity and *naïveté*. But, when Mr. G. H. Smillie produces his idyl called "In Connecticut," with its poetry of sunshine, of values, and of rustic life, we are confronted with the record of an impression which his own eyes have conveyed to his own heart—although it is needful to add, in the interests of complete veracity, that Mr. Smillie's charming picture represents his second manner rather than his first; and if, in Mr. Ogden Wood's pastoral of cattle "In the Open," some spectators may be inclined to trace the influence of Van Marcke—just as in Van Marcke's canvases the spirit of his master, Troyon, is echoed—the answer to the criticism is, in part, at least, that a composition so simple in its literary or story-telling aspects as two or three cows in a landscape very easily suggests the name of the man who handles it best. But the chief disadvantage under which the artist labors in being judged by the works of his first manner is, that very rarely do these works represent him as having penetrated, as the French say, into the fine substratum of things, *au fin fond des choses;* for it is when he tries so to penetrate that his true strength is discovered, and his true limitations are defined. It has been said of the French caricaturist Gavarni that he saw and knew nothing of the human body but its clothes; that the history of his time, as he wrote it, was only a well-dressed history; and that, when he descended into the saddest depths of the human heart, the light that he brought thither was a light without heat—a cold skepticism, not toward this man or that man, but toward the entire species. The test of an artist's work is the ability it discovers for penetrating the fine substratum of things, and for bringing to the examination of it a light that is both white and warm. In his "first manner" the artist is apt to be unduly concerned with mere means and instruments; with matters of technique, rather than with the things of the spirit. But it is the spirit that giveth life.

Mr. Frank D. Millet's "Cozy Corner," now in the Metropolitan Museum, is

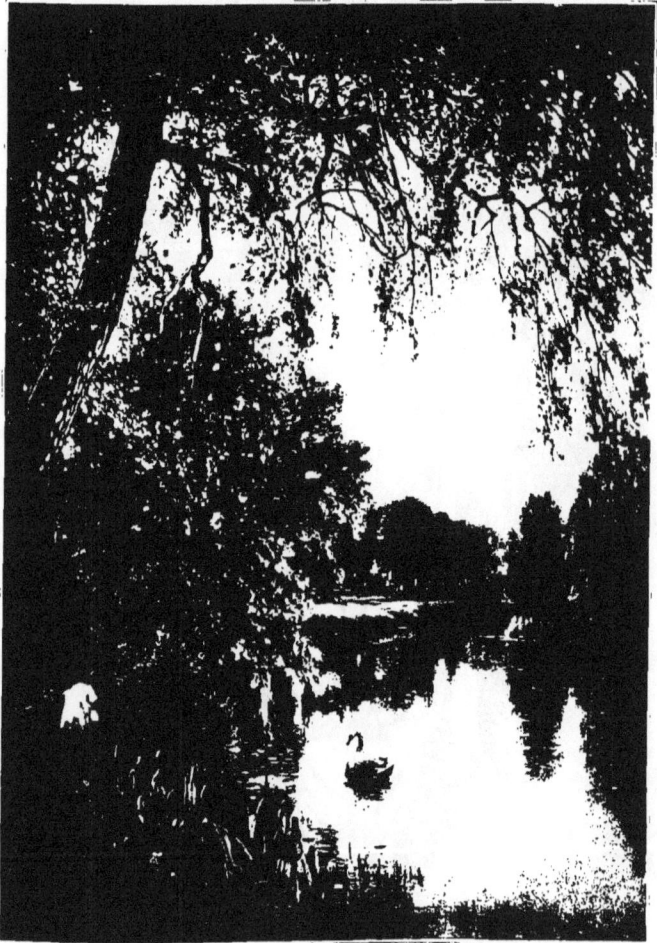

ERNEST PARTON : *The Swan's Paradise.*

not only one of the most charming compositions ever produced by that artist,
but one of the most interesting pictures of the new epoch of American art. In
showing no traces of the influence of Mr. Alma-Tadema, it exemplifies Mr. Millet's
first manner, and explains, in part, why this American artist has acquired a trans-

atlantic reputation. The grounds on which this reputation rests are described in a paragraph from a recent number of the London *Spectator*, à *propos* of a picture called " Piping Times of Peace," representing a man in a white waistcoat playing the fiddle in the presence of another man and a young woman. " The costume," says the *Spectator*, " is old-fashioned, the interior dark, the figures full of characteristic yet quiet life, the drawing good and easy, the color cool, harmonious, and pleasing. Such are the bare facts. What else may be said with certainty ? This, that the excellence of the picture depends on none of these excellences or details, but upon its general tone. It is hopeless to attempt, within our limited space, to dwell on this point, to try to explain our meaning to those who do not already possess some considerable knowledge of art. But, perhaps it is worth while to say that this excellence is one which may be seen in all the works of great artists of former times, and which is especially noticeable in all the Dutch schools. Peter de Hooge probably was the greatest master of tone in the world, and it is of a Peter de Hooge that Mr. Millet's ' Piping Times of Peace' reminds us. Over the whole picture, over the three figures, the chairs and tables, the walls and every detail, there is a lovely unity of subdued yet brilliant atmosphere, as if all that the artist had seen was, for him, appareled in celestial light, ' the beauty and the glory of a dream.' " But probably Mr. Millet himself would be content with reproducing the beauty of terrestrial light and of terrestrial tone, leaving " the light that never was on land or sea" to the dreams of those who lay much store by dreaming. One charm of Mr. Millet's " Cozy Corner" is its ease and unconventionalism of composition ; and he might himself have written that interesting little letter sent by his French namesake, Jean Francois Millet, to a friend : " I also have met a number of people who tell you, with a grave air, like that of a person who is disclosing something of fundamental importance, that ' you can't deny it ; there certainly are rules of composition.' And they have confidence in saying this, because they have really read it somewhere. As, for a long time, I have believed that composition is only a means of communicating to others as clearly and strongly as possible what is in one's mind, and that thinking alone is able to bring to light the means of accomplishing this end, you may judge of my embarrassment." It is not likely, however, that this mental condition produced any very serious disturbance. Mr. F. D. Millet's reputation has been steadily advancing since the appearance of the " Cozy Corner." Another example of a " first manner" is Mr. Edwin A. Abbey's young Puritan maiden on her way " Homeward," along a sandy stretch of sea-coast. Mr. Abbey has since become widely known as a student and interpreter of such English characters as are found

maria brooks — 1884

in Goldsmith's comedy "She Stoops to Conquer," and in old English songs, and his name is already associated with the madrigals of Robert Herrick and the sonnets of William Shakespeare. His claim to distinction lies in the fact that

Edwin A. Abbey : *Homeward.*

he possesses the ability to give us a kind of pleasure which no other artist gives us; a pleasure peculiar to himself; a pleasure which we feel we could never have experienced had it not come from him—for, as has been said of Botticelli,

GEORGE H. BOUGHTON : *The Page.*

he paints his subjects with an undercurrent of original sentiment which touches us as the real matter of the picture ; he blends the charm of story and sentiment with the charm of line and color—that is to say, the medium of the art of poetry with the medium of abstract painting ; and his morality is all sympathy. In Mr. Ernest Parton's "Swan's Paradise" we have another of his delightful transcripts of English rural scenery. It belongs to the same rank as the "Pond Lilies," already reproduced for this portfolio, and now in the collection of Mr. William T. Evans, where it appears under the name of "On the Arran, England." Mr. H. W. Robbins's "Mountain Road," with its pervasive sunshine, transparent shadows, and delicious distance, seems at first like a piece of out-doors, but the reader will fail to find in it any servile fidelity of minute detail. Mr. Brush's "Mourning her Brave" (in Mr. T. B. Clarke's collection) shows an Indian widow lamenting the husband whose dead body lies in the snow on the summit behind her. Mr. James M. Hart's cattle-piece, "Under the Trees," is, for some reasons, the most satisfactory of his canvases. It was presented to the Metropolitan Museum of Art by Mr. Cornelius Vanderbilt.

MARCUS-SIMONS : *A Fan.*

RIDGWAY KNIGHT : *French Washerwomen.*

V.

F. A. BRIDGMAN : *A Lady of Constantinople.*

THUS far I have mentioned certain causes of the present epoch of American art, and have illustrated their action by references to representative pictures. I have shown that our painters have gone to Europe, and especially to Paris, for purposes of study ; that they have there acquired a profound respect for the technique of their art taught in France ; that their efforts have found appreciation on this side of the Atlantic ; that in the city of New York alone there are now more than twenty private collections of American pictures ; that the establishment of the American Art Galleries by Mr. James F. Sutton, with its annual prizes of two thousand dollars each, has been an important service; that the National Academy of Design and the Society of American Artists have offered prizes and improved the quality of their administration; that the monthly exhibitions at the Union League Club, the Century Club, and similar institutions, together with the semi annual exhibitions of the Metropolitan Museum of Art, have provided unusual opportunities for the display of useful pictures under the most favorable auspices; that the Art Students' League has provided instruction by competent teachers fresh from the best foreign ateliers; that the erection of comfortable and even elegant studio-buildings has kept pace with the increasing needs; and that the best specimens of modern and classic art have found their way to our doors through the liberality of the American collector and amateur, notwithstanding the very oppressive import duties of thirty per cent of the cost-price. I have shown that through the operation of these causes the American art of the present epoch is different from that of any former epoch and superior to it, although still beset with the limitations of infancy; and that, in figure-painting particularly, it is realistic in the sense of being sympathetic with the true life and occupations of the people.

In saying that some of the best specimens of modern and classic art have found their way to our doors through the liberality of the American collector and amateur, one is reminded particularly of the recent magnificent pictorial acquisitions of the Metropolitan Museum of Art. That institution was founded in the year 1870, owing to a movement initiated by the Art Committee of the Union League Club, to whom had been referred a memorial from American citizens in Europe, suggesting the importance of early measures for the establishment of a metropolitan art museum. The committee, consisting of Messrs. George P. Putnam, J. F. Kensett, J. Q. A. Ward, W. Whittredge, George A. Baker, Vincent Colyer, and S. P. Avery, called a public meeting to consider the subject, and sent invitations to members of the National Academy of Design, the Institute of Architects, the New York Historical Society, and the leading clubs. Mr. William Cullen Bryant presided, and in his opening address declared that, if a tenth part of what was every year stolen from the city, under pretense of the public service, for the benefit of political rogues, were expended on a museum of art, we might have, in a spacious and stately building, collections formed of works left by the world's greatest artists which would be the pride of the country; we might possess an annual revenue which would bring to the museum every stray statue and picture of merit for which there should be no ready sale to individuals, every smaller collection in the country which its owner could no longer conveniently keep, every noble work by the artists of former ages which, by any casualty, after long re-

maining on the walls of some ancient building, should be again thrown upon the world.   But when the owner of a private gallery of art desired to leave his treasures where they could be seen by the public, he looked in vain for any insti-

H. W. WATROUS : *Holding the Fort.*

tution to which he could send them.   If a public-spirited citizen desired to employ a favorite artist upon some great historical picture, there were no walls upon which it could be hung in the public sight.   If a collection of works of art, made at great cost and with great pains, and perhaps during a lifetime, was for sale in Europe, we might find men in America willing to contribute to the purchase of it; but, were it brought hither, there was no edifice to give it hospitality. The little kingdom of Saxony, with an area less than that of Massachusetts, and a population but little larger, possessed a museum of the fine arts marvelously rich. Spain, a third-rate power in Europe, and poor besides, owned a museum of the fine arts the opulence and extent of which absolutely bewildered the visitor. Even Holland and Belgium, kingdoms almost too small to be heeded by the greater powers of Europe, had their public collections of art, which were the resort of admiring visitors from all parts of the civilized world. Moreover, we required an extensive public gallery to contain the greater works of our painters and sculptors. The American soil was prolific of artists. The fine arts blossomed not only in the populous regions of the United States, but even in its solitary places. Go where you would, into whatever museum of art in the Old World, and you found there artists from the New, contemplating or copying the masterpieces of art which they contained. Furthermore, our painters found their genius cramped by the narrow space in which they were constrained to exercise it, and were obliged to confine themselves for the most part to cabinet pictures for private dwellings, with little opportunity for that larger treatment of important subjects which a greater breadth of canvas would allow them, and by which the higher and nobler triumphs of their art had been achieved.

Were Mr. Bryant alive to-day, he would see the institution of which he was the first vice-president, and one of the most influential founders, in full possession of all the advantages that his eloquence so clearly depicted, with the single exception of great mural compositions, like those with which contemporaneous France has adorned the walls of the Pantheon in Paris. The Metropolitan Museum, though compelled to wait seventeen years for it, now finds itself in possession of a really valuable array of modern and classic pictures. Mr. Cornelius Vanderbilt deserves the credit of having set a contagious example by presenting the large and justly celebrated "Horse Fair" of Rosa Bonheur, which he purchased at the sale of the A. T. Stewart collection for more than fifty thousand dollars. Next came Mr. George I. Seney with twelve valuable and beautiful pictures, including landscapes by Messrs. George Inness, A. H. Wyant, and Charles H. Davis, an interior with figure (the "Cozy Corner," which we have already reproduced), by Mr. Francis D. Millet; the allegorical scene, "Mystery," by Mr. Carl Marr (also in this portfolio); the "Organ Rehearsal," by Lerolle; two examples of Josef Israels, and two of Anton Mauve. Only a few weeks afterward, Miss Catherine Lorillard Wolfe bequeathed her entire private collection of oil-paintings, containing canvases

WALTER GAY : *Asking a Blessing.*

by Meissonier, Gérôme, Knaus, Corot, Munkacsy, Troyon, Detaille, Gabriel Max,
Jules Breton, Sir Frederick Leighton, Cot, Rico, Schreyer, Bouguereau, Cabanel,
Vollon, and others, some of them of singular interest ; and this splendid gift has

been followed by that of Mr. Henry G. Marquand, who has presented to the museum a noble collection of old masters, which of itself is enough to make New York city an interesting place of art-study. All these treasures are in addition to the Cesnola Cypriote antiquities (which show the beginnings of Greek art), the Vanderbilt drawings by old masters, and the collections of ancient engraved gems, Greek pottery and porcelain, musical instruments, casts of Egyptian and Greek statues, modern statuary, ancient Greek, Roman, and Venetian glass, and Japanese lacquers; and to-day the museum may almost claim to have achieved the purpose for which it was established, namely—to combine the functions of the British National Gallery and the art departments of the British Museum and the South Kensington Museum; in other words, to collect and publicly exhibit adequate examples of the ancient and modern schools of painting and sculpture, and to provide as large and complete a collection as possible of objects which, without coming within the class just mentioned, derive their chief value from the application of fine art to their production—in short, a representative museum of fine art applied to industry.

The principal difficulty with which the museum has had to contend has arisen from its relation to the municipal authorities. "The local government," says Mr. John Taylor Johnston, its first and only president, "has leased to us a building, and makes an annual contribution toward the expenses of maintaining the museum, on the condition that we in return shall provide an exhibition of works of art and admit the public without charge. So far as pecuniary considerations are concerned, the contract is very largely a losing one on our side. The public receive the entire benefit of the institution, while we contributed in 1884 about thirty thousand dollars, and spend from fifteen thousand to thirty thousand dollars annually out of our funds as a free gift to enable them to receive that benefit. We, in fact, exhaust our entire income and large special subscriptions among ourselves each year in the mere expense of educating the public through our free exhibitions; and, as a result, we have no money for purchases, but depend wholly on the gifts of members for the increase of our art illustrations. These gifts have been of unexampled generosity." Another difficulty, described by the same authority, was due to a fierce attack upon General di Cesnola and his collection, which began in the year 1880, when the Cypriote antiquities were first completely arranged and exhibited. It was charged in the public prints that certain objects in the Cesnola collection had been fraudulently manufactured and deceptively restored. "General di Cesnola," says Mr. Johnston, in his annual review of the institution in 1884, "published a brief and total denial of the charges against

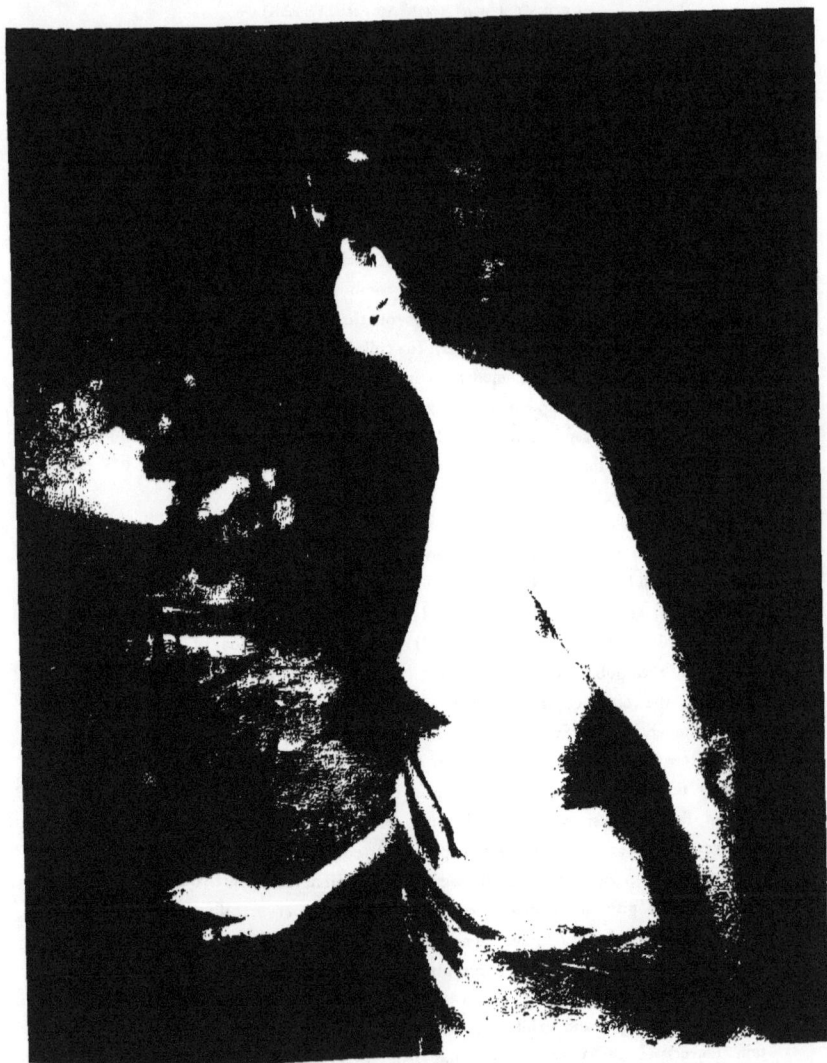

him and the collection; and addressed to us, and afterward to a committee of investigation appointed to examine into the accusations, full and explicit contradictions of each and every charge. The indignant language used by him in these three communications was made the subject of a libel-suit against him, in which the issues were distinct as to the truth or falsehood of the accusations against the director, the entire collection, and the specific objects in it. The jury gave patient and faithful attention during a protracted investigation for three months. Their findings, made February 2, 1884, sustained the entire integrity of the Cesnola

WILLIAM H. HOWE : *Normandy Bull.*

collection, established the baselessness of each and every one of the charges, and vindicated the director from the absurd accusation that he, the discoverer of the Cypriote antiquities, had made fraudulent objects and deceptive restorations." The future of the Metropolitan Museum now seems brilliant; and an examination of the condition of such institutions as the Cincinnati Art School and Museum, the St. Louis Museum of Art, the Art Institute of Chicago, the Art Museum of Detroit, the Cleveland Academy of Fine Arts, the Buffalo Library and Art Building, the Layton Art Gallery of Milwaukee, and other Western institutions, together with the Boston Museum of Fine Arts, the Philadelphia Academy of Fine Arts, the Peabody Institute in Baltimore, and the Corcoran Art Gallery in Washington—an examination, I say, of the present condition of these institutions would show much ground for congratulation and encouragement, as every one will agree who has read Mr. Ripley Hitchcock's interesting article in the *Century* magazine for August, 1886, on the Western art movement. From that paper the following facts have been gathered: Within six years preceding 1886 more than a million dollars were given to the museum and art-school of Cincinnati, and the names of more than four hundred pupils were entered on the books. The teachers were paid out of an annual income of fifteen thousand dollars from the Joseph Long-worth endowment fund, and the school building of blue limestone is the best of its kind in the United States, standing three hundred and fifty feet above the Ohio, combining Romanesque arches with gables and dormers in lighter vein, and having a ground-plan of eighty-two feet by one hundred and forty-one, and three stories, the first two with ten studios, and with generous rooms for primary, modeling, and wood-carving classes, and the third with a noble hall one hundred feet in length for classes in drawing from the cast and from the model. The new museum is Romanesque also, but, although two hundred and fourteen feet in length by one hundred and seven in breadth, it represents only the central pavilion and west wing of the original plan. The object of the instruction, in the words of the director, General A. T. Goshorn, is to secure training that will fit students for occupations requiring artistic skill, and to make practical applications of art to the ordinary uses of life. The St. Louis Museum has an unusually complete col-lection of casts and autotypes, and its paintings are intended, not to tell a story or tickle an idle fancy, but to teach something of artistic values and relations. The autotypes are reproductions of sketches, studies, and paintings by classic and modern masters; and more than a thousand carbon prints of collections in the British Museum, and five hundred sculptural and architectural casts, illustrate the historical development of art. Every year the director, Professor Ives, goes to Europe to study the latest results of the South Kensington system, the English potteries, and the Continental schools and museums. "The work to be done in the West," he says, "is not to bring French or other paintings before the public, but to make something out of the raw material. Nearly all the useful ores, especially iron, are found in Missouri. What the school and museum must help in is the working up of these ores with brains, so that the result shall be recog-nized, and a school founded like those of the Nuremberg and Belgian iron-workers." The Art Institute of Chicago, though destitute of large gifts of money

or collections, is attended by four hundred pupils, and has a building which, with
the land, represents a quarter of a million dollars. The galleries are occupied
chiefly by loan exhibitions, and there are nuclei of valuable collections of casts,

A. BISFORD McCLOSKEY : *Hydrangeas*.

autotypes, and paintings. The management of the Institute is vested in some of
the business men who have made Chicago what it is. In Milwaukee Mr. Frederick Layton has built a public art gallery, and there are many private art galleries.
In Minneapolis the Society of Fine Arts has established an academic school. In

Detroit the sum of one hundred and forty thousand dollars has been raised for an art-building, and ten thousand has been pledged for a collection of casts. Buffalo has recently erected a magnificent library and art-building, and the Cleveland Academy of Fine Arts has made an excellent beginning. But enough has been said to show that the wonderful story of the Metropolitan Museum of Art in New York city represents the general good-will of our wealthier classes toward the fostering of a national art.

To speak now of certain pictures that have been reproduced for this portfolio, the first thing that strikes the spectator of Mr. F. D. Millet's "On the Terrace" is the unconscious pose of the superb woman who leans against the white-marble wall. The painter introduces us, not to a model dressed and placed for the occasion, her expression paid for at so much an hour, and her impression that of artificiality itself, but to a woman of the classic days of Greece—a noble and superb type that might stand for the mother of the Gracchi. She is as beautiful as one of Homer's beautiful women, and the graceful folds of her white robes suggest those of the Greek statues in that hall of the Louvre which contains the Venus of Milo. Mr. Millet first exhibited this picture at the National Academy Exhibition in the city of New York in the spring of 1888, where it was bought by Mr. Edward D. Adams, whose interest in American art is attested by the fact that he has raised a fund of one hundred thousand dollars for its advancement. In Mr. Ridgway Knight's "French Washerwomen" a characteristic scene of country life in France has been faithfully interpreted. Six women on their knees are washing clothes in the river Seine, probably near the painter's home at Poissy, and an older one has started off with a large basket which a companion has helped to place on her shoulders. The air is full of summer sunshine, and the reflections of poplars and oaks are seen near the opposite shore. In the Riviera the women would be performing a similar service on the edge of a mountain-stream almost dried up; in Paris you would see them through the lattice-work of the great wash-houses that float on the Seine. But at Poissy the river flows near the tops of grassy banks, and the women wash their clothes in the open; and a very jolly set they are, younger and chattier than their sisters of the city or of the Riviera. The reader who remembers M. Zola's description, in L'Assommoir, of the Paris wash-house, where poor Gervaise chastised Virginie, will see how much happier are Mr. Knight's women, and will appreciate the fact, which has been mentioned before in connection with his pictures, that it is contented and prosperous children of the soil whom Mr. Knight finds within the borders of fair France.

The "Lady of Constantinople," which Mr. Bridgman paints, was bought by Mr. William T. Evans at the National Academy Exhibition of 1882. Like the figures in the same artist's picture of "Turkish Women," she is veiled, in accordance with the rules prescribed in the Koran; but, being a member of the upper

WALTER GAY : *The Spinners.*

class, the veiling is so lightly done that the features of her pretty face are not obscured. Were she a plebeian of the interior of Turkey, her entire face, except the eyes, would be concealed by a thick cloth. Mr. William T. Evans, it may be remarked, owns one of the finest collections of American pictures in the United States, and is one of the most discriminating and generous patrons of

American art. He contributed twenty-three examples to the great Loan Exhibition in the National Academy in 1883, for the benefit of the Bartholdi pedestal fund, and he has organized exhibitions in the Palma Club, Jersey City, which have led to the purchase of many American paintings. No collection of pictures in the State of New Jersey is so important as his. For years he has been a patron of the annual Artists' Fund Exhibition, having bought in 1887 not less than seven canvases at one sale. He lent half a dozen pictures to the first Louisville (Kentucky) Exhibition in 1883, which resulted in the establishment of a museum in that city. Recently he has added to his gallery an " F. S. Church room," with highly characteristic examples of that imaginative artist. Among the other painters represented in Mr. Evans's collection are Blakelock, Bristol, J. G. Brown, Brush, Bunner, Colman, De Haas, Dolph, Gaul, Gay, Winslow Homer, Hovenden, Inness, Eastman Johnson, Kensett, Louis Moeller, Thomas Moran, Murphy, Arthur Parton, Ernest Parton, Quartley, Shirlaw, Smedley, Tryon, Ulrich, and Wyant. He has acquired canvases also by Corot, Courbet, Constant, Daubigny, Delort, De Neuville, Edouard Frère, Jacque, Pasini, Schenck, Van Marcke, Vollon, Wahlberg, and Zügel, the total number being more than one hundred.

Mr. H. W. Watrous's " Holding the Fort" is a recollection of the days of the portable chair, or sedan. The attendant, left in charge of the vehicle, has entered it in a state of intoxication, and near by are evidences of some practical jokes that have been played upon him   Mr. Hamilton Hamilton's " Fetch it, Sir," shows a collie about to jump into the water at the dictation of his mistress, who has picked up a piece of a dead branch of a tree and will soon toss it upon the stream. The action of the dog is extremely happy, and the pose of the lady, who may be taken as a summer cottager on the bank of the Thames near Hammersmith, does not lack grace. As a piece of reproduction from an oil-painting, this picture deserves especial mention for its atmosphere and its values. It may almost be said to possess color.

Mr. Thomas Allen, whose " Thoroughbreds " was hung at the annual exhibition of the Society of American Artists in 1888, is a native of St. Louis, Mo., and a graduate of the Royal Academy of Fine Arts at Düsseldorf, in the master class of 1878. The teacher to whom he feels most indebted is Professor Dücker, the successor of Oswald Achenbach in the chair of Landscape Painting at that institution. "Dücker," says Mr. Allen, "is a man whose intimate and thorough knowledge of Nature, and strength as a painter, made his teaching a pleasure and an inspiration. He always sent his pupils to Nature for facts, and so made them independent investigators." Having taken the regular academic course at

WALTER GAY : *The Wigmaker.*

Düsseldorf, Mr. Allen turned his steps in the direction of France, and soon found himself in a charming cottage in the pretty village of Ecouen near Paris, where Edouard Frère painted for many years, and where Schenck and Chialiva still receive pupils.   He did not, however, enroll his name in the atelier of any master, although profiting much by association with M. Chialiva, whose knowledge of animal anatomy is widely recognized, and perfecting himself in composition by a careful study of the old Dutch masters in the Louvre. His first contributions to an American exhibition were at the National Academy in New York, whither he sent in 1877 his "Bridge at Lissingen," his "Harvest in the Eifel Mountains," and his "Street Scene at Carisbrooke"; and his first picture at the Paris *Salon* was "Evening in the Market-Place at San Antonio, Texas," in 1882. Two years previously he had been elected a member of the Society of American Artists; and in 1884 he became an associate of the National Academy.

Before beginning to paint a picture, Mr. Allen's habit is to solve the problem of light and shade, and arrangement, by composing his subject in charcoal on rough paper; so that, when taking his brush in hand, he does not grope, as the manner of many is. The necessities of our climate causing most of an artist's work to be done in-doors, Mr. Allen makes many a black-and-white composition during the long winter evenings, and thus utilizes by his method the hours which painters often consider unavailable; and, when summer comes, he proceeds to make detailed studies from Nature for every part of the picture which he expects to paint during the coming winter. The motive of the picture he invariably finds out-doors, and the execution is undertaken according to the methods just described. Mr. Allen has several hundred studies in his possession, some of them elaborated with the greatest care, others the briefest records of momentary impressions. He never mistakes style for thought, technique for subject-matter. He is a poet and a painter.

The "Normandy Bull" of Mr. William H. Howe is a study from life, and so are the "Hydrangeas" of Mrs. A. Binford McCloskey, whose flower-pieces at the annual exhibitions reveal evidences of the most painstaking and honest methods. It is not generally known that some specimens of the hydrangea measure thirty feet in circumference and bear more than a thousand heads of flowers on a single clump. Mr. Walter Gay made the greatest success of his life with the picture of the old peasant-woman "Asking a Blessing," at the Paris *Salon* of 1888. The delineation awakened praise in the studios, and secured for him a recognition in hundreds of new places. In the same spirit is "The Spinners," two aged French peasant-women in a humble abode, one at the wheel, the other looking on. A crucifix hangs behind them on the bare wall, suggesting the source of the peace that shines in their faces. Excellent is the action of "The Wigmaker," who, seated at his table, has just given to a wig a master-touch that intensely pleases its author. Most of Mr. Gay's professional friends would prefer him in the treat-

ment of such themes as these, because of the directness and simplicity of his expression and the sureness of his vision. His years in Paris and his studies under Bonnat have well served him in these recent efforts of his brush, because he here deals, not with the particular, but with the universal. The "Harvesters at Luncheon" of Mr. Ridgway Knight are three pretty women in the field, one holding a bowl of soup, another drinking water, and the third about to pour out some wine. A white cloth is spread upon the ground, and the empty luncheon-

RIDGWAY KNIGHT : *Harvesters at Luncheon.*

basket tells its own story. Plenty of sunshine, as usual, and graceful composition in the figures. This is the kind of scene that Mr. Knight enjoys reproducing, and that procured for him a gold medal at the Paris *Salon* of 1888, where the two young women, who stand on the bank of a river and beckon and call to the ferryman on the opposite shore, are the same interesting creatures who have been lunching.

Mr. Carleton T. Chapman's "White Wings," belonging to the collection of

Mr. Samuel T. Shaw, is a luminous pictorial effect, of which the motive may be seen any summer afternoon on the shores of Long Island Sound. The reflections of the yachts and larger vessels, and the vitalized whiteness of the sails, against which the afternoon sun is streaming, are skillfully rendered, and the indications are that the yachtsmen will have some sport. The composition of Mr. Chapman's picture has been studied in the interests of picturesqueness. The "Finding a Pose" is a fresh treatment by Mr. J. Louis Webb of a subject that artists often like to paint, with its draperies, rugs, furniture, *bric-à-brac*, and human figures. There sits the painter on a stool in his luxuriously appointed studio, chaffing the model, whose impersonation of Ceres, perhaps, has not yet found a pose in accordance with his desires. The goddess seems to have made a saucy reply which amuses her patron. The owner of this picture is Colonel Elliott F. Shepard.

A more important example of Mr. Richard Creifelds's talents than "The Sailor's Yarn" has not yet appeared. With the simplicity and directness of the "Playing Checkers," which we have already reproduced, it possesses the added trait of an indisputable Americanism. The characters were found in a tavern much frequented by sailors in the lower part of the city, and the principal speaker, whose right hand is in his trousers-pocket and whose left arm is extended in a gesture, might be seen any day in the New York haunts that American sailors frequent. His manner of wearing his hat and the easy unconventionalism of his posture are true and characteristic, and the expressions on the faces of his listeners reveal his success as a story-teller. It would not do to say that the five figures around the plain pine table might have been photographed from life, because their respective attitudes show the work of an artist; but this work has been so done that the effect is that of a scene directly from life. Mr. Creifelds does not find it needful to go to Europe for subjects. He discovers the picturesque close at hand, and he has a quick perception and a student's mastery of dominating traits.

Most of Mr. F. M. Boggs's professional life has been spent in France, because his ambition has been to perfect himself in the latest methods of Parisian technique; but, when he came to this city on a visit and painted for Mr. Thomas B. Clarke an American theme, he was able to express himself as fluently and successfully as if depicting the harbor of Havre. Here are the Statue of Liberty in the background, and, in the foreground, a sturdy little New York tug-boat bringing to her wharf, under some stress of weather, one of the largest of homeward-bound merchantmen. The wave-drawing is easy and sure, and the mastery of tone wonderful. This is a picture which pleases artists and the public alike; its story is clearly told and interesting, its technique is accomplished and even

ARTHUR PROTON : BD

brilliant. We may say of Mr. Boggs what the *Gazette des Beaux-Arts* has said of one of his European rivals, that he gives to the water movement, liquidity, and life; and, with happy talent, knows the spots where the sun's rays cross it to fill it with light.

Mr. Arthur Parton's "Harlem Bridge by Moonlight," with its western sky illumined at the horizon, its pale stars glimmering through the breaks in the clouds, its rows of lights across the structure, its distant house-tops, its tug-boat on the river, and its stretch of shore in the foreground, has the elements of a pleasing composition. The always difficult problem of painting moonlight so that its quality shall be its own, and not that of weakened sunlight, has been success-fully solved. This artist, indeed, does not search for easy tasks, nor does he repeat his subjects. Whether treating the Scottish Highlands, the Adirondack forests, or the suburban scenery of the metropolis, where most of his life has been spent, he displays the carefulness in draughtsmanship that he learned long ago of his master Mr. William T. Richards, and at the same time paints with a breadth that the great Philadelphian has certainly never seemed to overvalue. The "Confidence" of Mrs. Helen C. Hovenden was purchased by Mr. John Herriman, of New York city, for his private collection, where it hangs in such good company as that of Mr. Frederick Dielman's "Moro-Players." A young peasant-girl, holding a tin milk-can under her left arm, stands near a heifer around whose head is a leather band from which project long iron nails. Her right hand rests confidently upon the animal's neck. The two creatures trust each other.

Much more than a portrait is Mr. Frank Fowler's charming subject of a boy with a violin. As a composition, it won the attention of artists and amateurs at the exhibition of the Society of American Artists in 1888, and as a piece of painting it has a special interest of its own. After ten years of study in Paris, under M. Carolus-Duran and the late M. Cabanel, Mr. Fowler returned to the United States, took a studio in New York city, and proceeded to paint portraits. He had learned the best that Paris had to teach, not only in the ateliers of his masters, but also in the galleries of the Louvre; and, as the intention of this portfolio is to include some representative specimens of recent American portrait-ure, Mr. Fowler's boy with the violin well deserves its place. More "important" subjects he has undoubtedly exhibited: for example, his portrait of Samuel J. Tilden, in the Capitol at Albany; his portrait of the actress Helena Modjeska, now hanging in the library of her home in Poland; his portrait of Professor R. H. Bull, belonging to the University of the City of New York, and to be seen in the Council-Room of that institution on Washington Square; his portrait of Mrs. Frank Fowler, daughter of the late Bishop Odenheimer, of New Jersey, which

is treated as a *genre* motive and entitled "At the Piano"; and his portrait of the Rev. Horatio Nelson Powers, D. D., in the possession of that gentleman himself. But the "Portrait of a Boy with Violin" is in all respects a representative work of the artist, and, for some reasons, more interesting than any he has produced. The boy is a boy, in the first place, and he is not posing, and he is attractive personally; the violin is a violin, and it really belongs to the boy; and the *ensemble* is picturesque. Mr. Fowler has painted some notable *genres* as well the "Two Friends," owned by Mr. O. W. Buckingham; "In the Garden,"

HELEN C. HOWESON *Portrait*

owned by Mr. H. C. Howells; and "Pleasant Thoughts," owned by Mr. J. R. Haydon, of Janesville, Pennsylvania. The painter is a leading member of the Society of American Artists.

Miss Maria Brooks's "I wonder if he Really Means it?" tells a story akin to that of Mr. Millais's "Yes or No," but is entirely original in conception. The young woman in the picture has just received a love-letter, and her face and attitude express at least a condition of willingness. Miss Brooks has spent most of her professional life in England, and she brings to our art exhibitions an influence

FRANK FOWLER : *Portrait of a Boy with Violin.*

hitherto almost strange. She paints portraits, *genres*, and figure-pieces with equal cleverness. One of her most important portraits is that of the Rev. Morgan Dix, D. D., of Trinity Church, New York. We are indebted to Mr. Arthur W. Blake, of Boston, for permission to reproduce the noble classic figure of Chloe, by Mr. Henry O. Walker. Our readers will remember that Chloe was the surname of Ceres at Athens, and that her festival was celebrated annually with much rejoicing by the Greeks. The word itself denotes the fresh greenness of the young blade of corn, and also the golden yellow of the harvest. Mr. Thomas Hovenden is one of the few successful American painters who have studied in the Kensington Art School; but his subsequent Paris training has most in-fluenced his career, and it was to the Paris *Salon* that he sent the " Brittany Image-Seller " (now owned by Mr. William T. Evans) from his studio in that city.

THOMAS HOVENDEN : *A Brittany Image-Seller.*

RHODA HOLMES NICHOLLS : *The Scarlet Letter.*

VI.

F. D. MILLET : *A Reader.*

THE practice of holding special exhibitions of pictures, in addition to the regular annual exhibitions of the Academy, the Water-Color Society, the Society of American Artists, and the Etching Club, has done much in New York city and the country at large to foster American art; and, without attempting any complete catalogue of such exhibitions, it is now in place to note some of the more recent and influential of them. The largest of the many loan exhibitions in connection with the raising of funds for the erection of a pedestal for Bartholdi's Statue of Liberty Enlightening the World, was the one held in the National Academy of Design, New York, in December, 1883. It consisted of more than five thousand works of art—not only pictures, but sculptures, coins, armor and arms, stained glass, illuminated missals, musical instruments, faience and porcelains, tapestries and antique furniture, lacquers and laces, embroideries and costumes. " In assembling this rare and carefully selected loan collection," said the executive committee, " we believe that we have successfully accomplished a double task : first, in assuring the increase of a fund in which not one com-

munity alone, but the entire nation, should feel an interest; and also in awakening among us a potent influence in art.   To the Exhibition of 1876, in Philadelphia, the country owes an enormous debt of gratitude, not only for the bequest
of taste in things beautiful and refining to our homes, but for practical results in
fostering in America the remunerative industries of interior decoration and
adornment."   An interesting portfolio, containing original contributions from emi-
nent artists and men of letters, was prepared and offered for sale.   One of its
articles was a sonnet by the late Emma Lazarus, which addressed the Statue as
the Mother of Exiles, from whose beacon-hand glowed a world-wide welcome:

> " Keep, ancient lands, your storied pomp," cries she,
>   With silent lips.   " Give me your tired, your poor,
>   Your huddled masses, yearning to breathe free;
>   The wretched refuse of your teeming shore;
>   Send these, the homeless, tempest-tossed to me:
>   I lift my lamp beside the golden door."

The failure of the supply of Millets, Corots, Rousseaus, and other members
of the Fontainebleau school, led a Paris art-dealer, M. Durand-Ruel, to bring to
this country, in 1886, a collection of works by the so-called Impressionists.   When
the former painters first appeared, he said, the artists, critics, and amateurs cried
out against them in angry chorus; but to-day their pictures had reached fabulous
prices, and amateurs bought, for more than their weight in gold, paintings that
they would hardly deign to look at a few years ago; while, to meet the incessant
demand, search had been made far and wide for every vestige of their skill   But
the Impressionists, he claimed, were the worthy successors of those great men,
although amateurs accustomed to the black and bituminous tones of the latter
school were sometimes frightened by the boldness of handling and the tonal
clearness of the new painters.   And when asked to explain just what the Impressionists tried to do, and in what they differ from other artists, he quoted a
French critic to the effect that their immediate fathers were Corot, Courbet, and
Manet, to whom painting owes its deliverance from " bitumen, chocolate-brown,
tobacco-juice, and the rest of the studio tricks," and its perception of the most
delicate shades of colors, and of the true relation between the atmosphere which
lights the picture and the tone of all the objects contained in it.   " Go for a
walk," continued this critic, " along the banks of the Seine, at Asnières, for
instance; your eye takes in at one view the red-tiled roof and the shining white
wall of a cottage, the tender green of a poplar, the yellow of the road, and
the blue of the river.   At noon, in the summer, the whole coloring of the land-

scape will appear to you raw, glaring, without the least gradation, and without
the veil of a general half-tone.   Before the arrival among us of the Japanese
picture-books, there was no one in France who dared to seat himself on the

BURR H. NICHOLLS : *By the Roadside.*

banks of a river and to put side by side on his canvas a roof frankly red, a
whitewashed wall, a green poplar, a yellow road, and blue water! Before the
day of Japan this was impossible. The painter told nothing but lies."   What

the Impressionists did, therefore, was to borrow from Corot, Courbet, and Manet
their honest way of painting in the open air, off-hand, with vigorous touches,
and from the Japanese their bold and novel methods of coloring. The exhibition
in New York caused great interest on the part of both artists and amateurs; and
many of the canvases—particularly the luminous landscapes of Claude Monet—
found a way into the private collections. To-day, three years afterward, the
fame of Monet is well established, and his pictures are displayed in the galleries
of the most fashionable dealers. Among the earliest buyers in this country was
Mr. Albert Spencer, the sale of whose collection of sixty-eight modern French
paintings in February, 1888, was the most notable art-event of the season.

Mr. Herbert Herkomer excited some interest in November, 1882, by his exhibition of oil or water-color portraits of John Ruskin, Archibald Forbes, Joseph
Joachim, Hans Richter, and others, at Mr. Knoedler's gallery, together with about
fifty etchings and mezzotints. The artist published a catalogue with notes by
himself, having "invariably found that the art-loving public want to know what
a painter has to say about his own work"; but much of what he had to say
was gossip about his celebrated sitters. Mr. Herkomer painted a number of
portraits of Americans during his stay in this country, and at very remunerative
prices. One of his most characteristic works is the portrait of Mr. Whitelaw
Reid, which hangs in the drawing-room of the Lotos Club. In the "notes" he
declares that "more nonsense has been written and talked about etching than
about any other form of art," and that "nothing is more deplorable than the
tendency of the present day to *scribble* on copper." He adds that he can not
detect the "slightest difference in the artistic sensation when copying my own
work or that of another man. In both cases the picture has to be reduced, re-
proportioned in its tones, and interpreted from the engraver's point of view."
This would be pleasant reading for our wood-engravers, to whom some persons
are inclined to deny a distinct rank as creative artists. Other foreign painters,
whose works were seen at special exhibitions, were M. Munkacsy, with his
"Christ before Pilate," and "Christ on Calvary"; Karl von Piloty, with his
"Wise and Foolish Virgins"; Hans Makart, with his "Diana's Hunting Party";
Eugène Delacroix, with his "Death of Sardanapalus," and his "Interior of a
Dominican Monastery in Spain"; M. Puvis de Chavannes, with nine examples,
exclusive of reductions of his mural paintings at the Pantheon; M. Charles
Méryon, with about one hundred and forty original drawings and etchings; and
J. M. W. Turner, with his "Liber Studiorum," exhibited at the Grolier Club,
January, 1888.

CHARLES C. CURRAN

The second annual exhibition of the Painters in Pastel was held in Mr.
Wunderlich's gallery in May, 1888, and contained works by Carroll Beckwith,
R. F. Blum, Lyell Carr, W. M. Chase, W. A. Coffin, Kenyon Cox, Herbert
Denman, Miss Caroline T. Heeker, John La Farge, F. C. Jones, W. L. Palmer,

FREDERIC REMINGTON — From a Buffalo Bill poster

J. H. Twachtman, Irving R. Wiles, Alden Weir, and J. Louis Webb. These artists are among the most vigorous and masculine of their profession, and they are charmed with this medium of drawing, not because the results are like velvet to the eye, but because "de la beauté le pastel a l'éclat et la fragilité"—because pastel has the *éclat* and the fragility of beauty.

Of unique interest was the exhibition in the Union League Club, April, 1888, of the work of the women-etchers of America. It consisted of more than five hundred examples, collected originally by the print department of the Boston Museum of Fine Arts, and most of them were painters' etchings, as distinguished from reproductive etchings. The first American woman who used the etching-needle was Miss Cole, sister of the great didactic landscapist, Thomas Cole, and several of her plates, bearing the date of 1844, were displayed by the art-committee of the Club. Twenty-five years afterward Mrs. Greatorex revived the art among her sisterhood by producing the "Old Tavern in Bloomingdale"; and there are already several American women whose reputation in this particularly attractive though modest department of the fine arts exceeds that of any other women in any part of the world.

Exhibitions of the works of a single painter, either after his death or previous to his departure for Europe, are of frequent occurrence, and the catalogues prepared for them often contain interesting biographical or critical sketches. Fifty-seven oil-paintings of Mr. George Inness—among them his famous "Niagara Falls" and "Mount Washington"—were gathered and shown by the American Art Association in April, 1884, Mr. Ripley Hitchcock writing a prefatory essay, in which he quoted Mr. Inness as saying: "Long before I ever heard of Impressionism, I had settled to my mind the underlying laws of what may properly be called an impression of nature. And I felt satisfied that whatever is painted truly according to any idea of unity will, as it is perfectly done, possess both the subjective sentiment—the poetry of nature—and the objective fact sufficiently to give the commonest mind a feeling of satisfaction, and through that satisfaction elevate to an idea higher than its own. Just as I have fought pre-Raphaelitism, I fight what I consider the error of what is called Impressionism." Forty-four oil-paintings, by Birge Harrison and Alexander Harrison, were exhibited in January of the same year. A biographical preface directed attention to the fact that these two brothers, after studying at the École des Beaux-Arts, went to the extreme western end of France, and devoted themselves in the seclusion and quietude of Pont-Aven to a serious study of out-of-door nature, "entirely apart from French influences; trying to see nature with their own eyes, and to grasp and

render it after their own fashion. There has been prevalent in America," continued the writer, " a general impression to the effect that all American artists
working abroad are only the weakened reflections of stronger foreign painters ;
that their work is of necessity only imitative in aim and character. To a certain

STANLEY MIDDLETON : *Telling her Fortune.*

limited extent this is perhaps so, but it is much less true than has been generally
supposed, as is evinced by the fact that the foremost French critics and amateurs
have all the time been praising their work for its freshness and originality. At
the *Salon* of 1882, the American display was, as a whole, so remarkable for this

quality that the critics of *l'Art*, the *Gazette des Beaux-Arts*, and other prominent French periodicals, came forth in frank and enthusiastic praise of the school of young foreigners who were thus introducing into the *Salon* a new and original style of painting. *L'Art* concluded a long and appreciative article with the cry of ' Hail Columbia' ! " Fifty-three landscapes by Mr. Charles H. Davis, an artist of a singularly poetic temperament, who, in his works, discovers nothing to remind one of his masters, M. Boulanger and M. Lefebvre, were exhibited in March, 1887. The catalogue briefly announced that Mr. Davis had exhibited in the *Salon* since 1881, and that at the Second Prize-Fund Exhibition in New York he received one of the gold medals of honor. One hundred and thirty sketches, studies, and pictures, by the promising and lamented William Bliss Baker, were exhibited at about the same time—the preface to the catalogue saying that all Mr. Baker knew of art he learned from American sources, and that the tidings of his untimely death, at the early age of twenty-seven, would be received with sincere regret by all who took an intelligent interest in the growth of native American art; that the young artist was animated by an intense love of nature, which he manifested from his earliest years, and that this, aided by his great industry and energy, was among the chief elements of his success. His illness, which he bore with singular fortitude, was very long and painful, and was caused by an injury to the spine through a fall on the ice while skating. Seventy-one drawings by Mr. Edwin A. Abbey, illustrating Goldsmith's comedy " She Stoops to Conquer," were exhibited by the Grolier Club, in December, 1886. The catalogue contained essays by Mr. Henry James, Mr. George William Curtis, and Mr. W. Mackay Laffan. Mr. James found that " no one has ever understood breeches and stockings better than Mr. Abbey, or the human leg, that delight of the draughtsman, as the costume of the last century permitted it to be known. The petticoat and bodice of the same period have as little mystery for him, and his women and girls have altogether the poetry of a by-gone manner and fashion. They are not modern heroines, with modern nerves and accomplishments, but figures of remembered song and story, calling up visions of spinet and harpsichord that have lost their music to-day, high-walled gardens that have ceased to bloom, flowered stuffs that are faded, locks of hair that are lost, love-letters that are pale. The spirit of the dramatist has passed completely into the artist's sense, but the spirit of the historian has done so almost as much. Mr. Abbey has evidently the tenderest affection for just the old house and the old things, the old faces and voices, the whole irrevocable human scene which the genial hand of Goldsmith has passed over to him, and there is no inquiry about

F. D. MILLET : *The Toilet.*

them that he is not in a position to answer. He is intimate with the buttons of coats, and the buckles of shoes; he knows not only exactly what his people wore, but exactly how they wore it, and how they felt when they had it on."

Mr. Laffan declared that in these drawings Mr. Abbey had "possessed himself of that imperial maiden who has reigned in prose and verse ever since William of Stratford wrote about her, down to her death at the hands of certain modern versifiers. She is the maiden whom Herrick loved, and to whom there is good reason to fear that Sir John Suckling made advances. Sometimes she has a milk pail, and oftener is dressed in silk; but she is the same wholesome and perfect femininity throughout, going a-Maying in May, full of laughter and awful provocations, and in October all tears and grave compunctions. All manner of men have set their ambitions on her since, from Mr. Tennyson in his trade, to Sir John Millais in his; but she has eluded them all to throw herself, without a reservation, into the arms of a young American. Mr. Abbey, saturated with all there is of English poetry behind Wordsworth, but with none that has been since, went afield in England sensitized beyond easy understanding to all the traditions of English sky and meadow, brook and copse, town and crumbling village. 'His girl,' as Herrick would have styled her, made him one with all her people, and taught him how they wore their clothes and their daily circumstances. This chain of happy figures, from the earliest hint of Herrick down to 'Sally in our Alley,' breathes from end to end the purest spirit and truest humanity of English poetry." In the "Homeward" of Mr. Abbey, reproduced in an earlier part of this portfolio, will be found the promise of his present fame.

Before leaving the subject of exhibitions, as related to the growth of American art, special mention should be made of that notable exhibition of "the private collection of paintings exclusively by American artists," owned by Mr. Thomas B. Clarke, which was made at the American Art Galleries from December 28, 1883, to January 12, 1884, for the benefit of a permanent fund for a prize to be given annually for the best American figure composition shown at the National Academy of Design. This collection, consisting at that time of one hundred and forty examples, though now much larger, was and is the oldest, most interesting, and most important of its kind in the country. In a prefatory note to the catalogue Mr. Clarke announced that he had purchased these pictures, representing many different methods and ideas, because he found something in each to please or instruct; he liked the pictures when he bought them; he had lived with them, and he liked them still; and it would give him sincere pleasure if the visitors to the Exhibition should enjoy the collection of the works of their countrymen as he himself had done. Mr. S. R. Koehler, in an introductory essay, described the Exhibition as undoubtedly the first of its kind ever held

here or anywhere else—an exhibition of purely American works—(works, that is
to say, done by artists either born or resident in the country), publicly exposed
for a purpose conducive to the advancement of art in the United States, and
brought together not for the sake of ostentation but for the collector's own en-
joyment, and in obedience to the dictates of that love of art which irresistibly
compels those possessed by it to surround themselves with artistic objects. Mr.
Koehler asserted that, although for years more and more attention had been paid
in this country to European art, especially by the professional collector, there

ARTHUR PARTON : *In the Month of May.*

was a decided turning toward home art. The best proof of this was to be
found in the loan exhibitions, where, only a short time previously, the works of
our own painters were but sparingly seen, and the few that did appear were
principally contributed by the artists themselves. The pride of the owners, as
well as the success of the exhibitions, he continued, seemed to demand that the
works of only foreign artists should be shown; but the Loan Exhibition of 1882,
at the Metropolitan Museum, had clearly demonstrated that a revolution had set
in. The Council of the National Academy sent a letter to Mr. Clarke, accept-

ing, with great pleasure, his most liberal offer to endow a yearly prize of three hundred dollars, and promising to administer the trust in the best interests of art. "The progress made of late years," said the Council, "by artists in all fields of labor is a matter for hearty congratulation, while such generous and enlightened recognition and assistance as you now offer, and have already given in other ways, can not but hasten the time when our great metropolis shall be as pre-eminent in the arts as in all other forms of industry and genius."

To digress for a few moments with references to individual pictures here reproduced, Mrs. Rhoda Holmes Nicholls's "Scarlet Letter" first claims attention. Hester Prynne, a favorite subject for artists' pencils, appears very much as Hawthorne describes her: "On the breast of her gown, in fine red cloth, surrounded with an elaborate embroidery and fantastic flourishes of gold thread, was the letter A, so artistically done that it had all the effect of a last and fitting decoration to the apparel which she wore. The young woman was tall, with a figure of perfect elegance on a large scale. She had dark and abundant hair, so glossy that it threw off the sunshine with a gleam, and a face which, besides being beautiful from regularity of feature and richness of complexion, had the impressiveness belonging to a marked brow and deep black eyes. She was lady-like, too, after the manner of the feminine gentility of those days" (about two hundred years ago, at Salem, Massachusetts); "characterized by a certain state and dignity, rather than by the delicate, evanescent, and indescribable grace which is now recognized as its indication. But the point which drew all eyes, and, as it were, transfigured the wearer—so that both men and women, who had been familiarly acquainted with Hester Prynne, were now impressed as if they beheld her for the first time—was that SCARLET LETTER, so fantastically embroidered and illuminated upon her bosom. It had the effect of a spell, taking her out of the ordinary relations with humanity, and inclosing her in a sphere by herself. In all her intercourse with society, there was nothing that made her feel as if she belonged to society. The poor, whom she sought out to be the objects of her bounty, often reviled the hand that was stretched forth to succor them. Dames of elevated rank were accustomed to distill drops of bitterness into her heart; sometimes through that alchemy of quiet malice, by which women can concoct a subtile poison from ordinary trifles, and sometimes, also, by a coarser expression, that fell upon the sufferer's defenseless breast like a rough blow upon an ulcerated wound. Hester had schooled herself long and well; she never responded to these attacks, save by a flush of crimson that rose irrepressibly over her pale cheek, and again subsided into the depths of her bosom." With an artist's privilege, Mrs.

Nicholls has painted her scene of "The Scarlet Letter" in Ellenville, Ulster County, New York, a village which did not have a railroad until a few years ago, and which is doubtless more in keeping with the sentiment of Hawthorne's story than

CHARLES C. CURRAN : *Spring Sunshine.*

the modern Salem. Mrs. Nicholls took a gold medal at the Prize Fund competition of the American Art Association for a large autumn landscape with figure, entitled "Those Evening Bells," which has since been published as an etching. She won a silver medal at the Triennial Exhibition in Boston, in 1884, for a picture of Venice which was bought by the Art Committee. She took the Queen's scholarship in London, and is a member of the "Società degli Acquarellisti" in Italy. She has painted in this country about five years. In her beautiful Venetian sketches she discovers a fine sense of what Mr. Ruskin would call the preciousness of the luminous sky.

Mr. Julius L. Stewart's "Portrait of Mme. la Comtesse de G——," which was hung at the *Salon* of 1887, has the true patrician air, and, however short-lived may be the artistic predilections of the day, will retain its interest as long as it and our civilization last. This brilliant young painter has sought the essential and has found it. How different his lot from that of Jean François Millet, who, on his death-bed, lamented to his friends that he was dying too soon, at an hour when he was only beginning to see clearly into nature and into art! In Mr. George D. Brush's "Before the Battle" an aged chief is giving his parting directions to a company of ardent braves. The subject, like the "Mourning her Brave," in an earlier part of this portfolio, discloses dramatic interest, and dexterity in the reproduction of textures. Mr. Percy Moran's "Knights of Old" was in the National Academy Exhibition of 1888, where Mr. George Vassar, Jr., purchased it for his private collection. A society woman is reading to her young daughter some stories about famous knights and the days of chivalry. This artist has no trouble in escaping the trivialities of prose while keeping faithful to the truth. Mr. Francis D. Millet's two figure-subjects serve but to emphasize the impression that he is a man of genius. Mr. Gilbert Gaul's "Taking the Ramparts," otherwise known as "Charging an Earthwork," is the most important and impressive of his battle-pieces of the civil war. It was hung in the South Gallery of the National Academy during the Exhibition of 1888. The reader will not fail to notice that Mr. Gaul is a painter of original methods and great success, although he has never studied an hour in Europe. He is one of the two or three Americans whose brush-work possesses style and distinction, but whose sojourn has continuously been in the United States; and it is his brother artists, after enjoying a course of European training, who most cordially testify to this style and distinction. Mr. Ridgway Knight's "Inventor," from the collection of Mr. W. H. Tailer, is in manner earlier than that of his other works here reproduced. The "Canova" of Mr. Marcius-Simons may be called a pendant to the "Young Lulli"; his "Sarah Bernhardt as La Tosca" represents the actress in her celebrated impersonation of the heroine in Sardou's well-known drama. The "Priscilla" of Miss Elizabeth Gardner, also from Mr. W. H. Tailer's collection, is an excellent example of her remarkable talents and of the influence of her master, Bouguereau. Mr. Burr H.

Nicholls's "By the Roadside," a study of sunshine and the open air, hangs in the private gallery of John S. White, LL. D., of New York city. Mr. C. C. Curran's "Evening in the Studio" is a characteristic sketch of artist-life in the metropolis in post-Bohemian days. The half-starved horses and riders of Mr. Frederic Remington's "Return of a Blackfoot War Party" tell a story of Indian hardships under the most benign government in the world. Mr. Remington recites what he has seen, but his splendid reputation as an illustrator for the magazines has

F. F. DE CRANO : *Rocher Rouge, Mentone.*

failed to satisfy the ambition of an artist who bids fair to become equally established as a professional painter. Mr. Thomas B. Clarke owns Mr. Stanley Middleton's "Telling her Fortune," that interesting young woman, with a pale-green hat and a seal-brown jacket trimmed with yellowish-white fur, who is examining the tea-grounds in the bottom of a porcelain cup. The artist has studied in the Paris schools under Dagnan-Bouveret, Benjamin Constant, and others, and has exhibited in the *Salons* of 1877, 1878, 1885, and 1887. He is a member of the Salmagundi Club. "In the Month of May," by Mr. Arthur Parton, with its blossoming apple-orchard, is a poem and pæan of spring. Its spirit is akin to that of Mr. C. C. Curran's "Morning Sunlight," from the collection of Mr. Samuel T. Shaw. The painter of the "Rocher Rouge, Mentone," Mr. F. F. de Crano, was born of French parents forty-five years ago, and came to America after studying in Paris and in London. He renewed his studies under Professor Schussele in the life-schools of the Pennsylvania Academy of Fine Arts, and showed his first important picture at the Centennial Exhibition, in 1876, at Philadelphia. His home is in a beautiful region of Delaware County, Pennsylvania, but he spends a great part of his time in the Riviera of southern France and Italy, where the sketch for the "Rocher Rouge" was made. The precipitous wall of rock marks the boundary between France and Italy, and is a conspicuous feature in the landscape around Mentone.

Mr. F. W. Freer has for several years sent to the annual exhibitions works that belong to the order of the purely poetic. They have poetry of line, poetry of tone, and poetry of thought. Most of them are figure-pieces in which a beautiful woman of the fashionable set exploits herself with results that make many of the compositions of Alfred Stevens seem tame; and none of them is more representative of his happiest efforts than "In the Looking-Glass," where we see a woman whom Mr. Howells and Mr. James have described a score of times for the delectation of hundreds of thousands of readers. Mr. Freer, a native of Chicago, studied art at the Munich Academy, and is a member of the Society of American Artists. The picture is owned by Mr. Thomas B. Clarke. A subject of a different import is the "Settling Up" of Mr. Henry W. Watrous, belonging to Mr. J. Osborne Moss. Some aristocratic gamblers, after a night session at Monte Carlo, are engaged in figuring out the financial position in which they stand to one another. Born in San Francisco, Mr. Watrous came to New York in 1864 at the age of seven years, and soon began to take lessons of Mr. Humphrey Moore, with whom he went to Spain in 1881. The next year he became a pupil of the École Bonnat, and, on the breaking up of that institution, studied with Jules Lefebvre and Gustave Boulanger. He exhibited his "Café Noir" in the *Salon* of 1884, and his "L'Addition" in the *Salon* of 1885. After a brief visit to the United States, he spent the winter of 1887 in Munich and Florence, and on returning to his native land in 1888 was elected a member of the Art Committee of the Union League Club. Mr. Watrous is already a *genre* painter of distinction on both sides of the Atlantic. His technique is so accomplished as to be always interesting of itself. He paints with equal love and with unusual ease a woman's expressive face and the legs of a Louis Seize chair. He

respects his subject, whatever it may be, and he discloses in his results the pleasure
with which they were produced.   Mr. Henry W. Parton's "Queen of the Garden" is a study of roses that delights the eye, and Mr. Carl Hirschberg's "Inter-

FREDERICK W. FREER   *In a Looking-glass.*

esting Item" presents a country damsel in the act of reading a paragraph in a
newspaper—an announcement of a marriage, perhaps.   The "Sunday Morning in
Old Virginia" represents the pious possibilities of the American negro during the
days of slavery.   It belongs to the collection of Mr. William T. Evans.

To return now to the subject of collectors and exhibitions, I am indebted to Mr. S. P. Avery for some historical notes, prepared originally for Lossing's "History of New York City." These notes were revised by Mr. Avery in 1885 for private circulation in pamphlet-form, and again revised in 1889 by Mr. S. P. Avery, Jr., for "Recent Ideals of American Art."

Fifty years ago the sale of paintings was mainly confined to the works of old masters, or copies from them. Dr. Hosack was an early collector of such canvases, and Gulian C. Verplanck was another. One of the earliest and best patrons of American art was Luman Reed, who gave to Cole a commission for the series of pictures entitled the "Course of Empire," now in the galleries of the New York Historical Society. At that time five hundred dollars was considered a very extravagant price for an oil-painting. Mr. William H. Aspinwall gathered a collection of old and modern works, which was recently sold by auction. Mr. William P. Wright bought Rosa Bonheur's "Horse Fair," and Mr. Marshall O. Roberts and Mr. August Belmont built private galleries. Mr. Boker established on Broadway the "Düsseldorf Gallery," with examples of Achenbach, Hubner, and other German artists, which caused a large importation of German canvases. Mr. Bryan, a public-spirited man of large means, gathered an interesting collection of the various schools of old art. These he tried in vain to give away to any city or public institution that would house and care for them. Finally, he died in 1870, and his pictures were consigned to the silent rooms of the Historical Society, buried and decaying.

The auction-sale of the collection of Mr. James M. Burt, in the panic times of 1857, proved that works of art were a good investment. In 1863 came the sale of Mr. John Wolfe's collection—French, German, Flemish, Dutch, and a few English and American pictures. They realized $114,000, an amount never before reached in this country, and for many years unsurpassed. In 1876 the galleries of Mr. John Taylor Johnston, who for twenty years had been a most generous patron, were vacated. The collection consisted of a hundred and ninety-one works in oil, a hundred and thirty-two in water-colors, and some marble statues. The artists of various nations were included in this famous gathering, and the proceeds were the unprecedented sum of $328,286, Church's "Niagara" bringing the highest price, $12,500. The hundred and ninety-one oil-paintings brought an average of $1,712, the highest yet reached at any sale in this country. In 1877 the R. M. Olyphant collection of paintings, exclusively by American artists, fetched $43,620, Kensett's "Autumn on Lake George" selling for $6,350. In 1868 the late Governor Latham's (of California) collection of eighty-three pictures brought

$101,205; a Gérôme, the largest amount, $5,500. In 1879 the joint collections of Messrs. Sherwood and Hart fetched $77,980, a Knaus reaching $3,300. In the same year Mr. Albert Spencer sold seventy-one paintings for $82,500, a Gérôme bringing $6,000. In 1880 the Nathan collection brought $30,117; a Bouguereau, $6,600. The same year Mr. J. Abner Harper sold a hundred and forty-four works for $106,790, a Van Marcke obtaining $3,725. In 1882 a part of the collection of Messrs. Morton and Hoe sold for $50,570; one by Regnault brought $5,900. In 1883 sixty-six pictures belonging to Mr. J. C. Runkle sold

HENRY W. WATROUS : *Settling Up.*

for $66,195; one by Millet for $3,850. The fact that during these years thirty-four collections of works of art, sold at auction by Messrs. Leeds, Somerville, Leavitt, and other auctioneers, under the direction of Mr. Avery, were disposed of for $1,427,870, will give an idea of the extent of the art trade. The highest price then paid at auction was for Church's "Niagara," bought for the Corcoran Gallery. At the Blodgett sale his "Heart of the Andes" brought $10,000. Mr. James G. Bennett paid for a small Meissonier, eight by ten inches, at the Johnston sale, $11,500; at the same sale Turner's "Slave-Ship" brought $10,000.

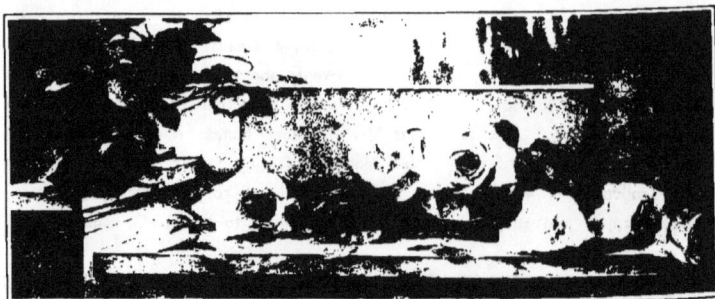

HENRY W. PARTON : *The Queen of the Garden.*

At Mr. John Wolfe's second auction, in 1882, a Bouguereau sold for $10,100. The house of Messrs. George A. Leavitt & Co. sold, in 1871, the Alexander White collection for $91,000, and, in 1872, Legrand Lockwood's gallery for $76,520, a Bierstadt bringing $5,100. The same year a portion of the gallery of Mr. Belmont brought $52,250

C. HIRSCHBERG : *An Interesting Item.*

ROBERT WICKENDEN : *The Approach of Evening.*

VII.

EDWARD H. POTTHAST : *A Brittany Girl.*

THE next picture-sale of importance (to continue the list already begun) was that of the Everard collection in 1873, which brought $96,480. This sum was not exceeded until nine years later, when Mr. John Wolfe disposed of his collection of eighty-two works for $131,815, although meantime the Newcombe collection had been sold for $34,900, the Maynard collection for $49,000, the Reid collection for $70,650, and the Coale collection for $71,477. In 1883 the J. C. Runkle collection brought $66,195, the number of canvases being sixty-six. Two important sales in 1885 were those of the George Whitney collection of two hundred and twenty-seven works, for $73,625, and the George I. Seney collection of two hundred and eighty-five works, for $406,600; but these figures soon paled in the presence of the

$1,205,503 obtained in 1886 for the Mary Jane Morgan collection of two hundred
and forty pictures. At this sale Sir Donald Smith, of Montreal, paid $45,500
for the "Communicants" of Jules Breton—the largest price ever bid for an oil-
painting at public auction in the United States up to that time, and exceeded since
only by the $60,000 paid for Meissonier's "1807," and the $53,000 paid for Rosa
Bonheur's "Horse Fair" at the A. T. Stewart sale in 1887. The E. D. Morgan
collection of one hundred and fifty-one pictures brought $85,093, and the Rogers
and Bookwalter collection of one hundred and forty-four pictures, $67,994, in 1866.
Two notable events the next year were the dispersion of the Richard H. Halstead
collection of sixty-five pictures and the A. T. Stewart collection of two hundred
and seventeen pictures, the former bringing $84,320 and the latter $575,079. The
Henry Probasco collection of one hundred and two pictures, sold the same year,
was notable for the number of its early examples of the Fontainebleau school,
some of which were exhibited at the Universal Exposition in Paris in 1889, notably
Millet's celebrated canvas representing two farmers bringing home a young calf on
a litter. In 1888 the Albert Spencer collection of sixty-eight pictures, mostly of
cabinet size, and of the best period of the Fontainebleau school, brought $284,025,
a drove of cattle by Troyon fetching $26,000. The same year the Mott and
Kearney collection of one hundred and thirty-five works obtained $130,590; and
the next year the Thomas A. Howell collection of sixty-five pictures brought
$74,880, and the James H. Stebbins collection $162,550, the "Lost Game" of
Meissonier fetching $26,300.

Some very valuable old masters have recently been bought for American collections at enormous prices. Mr. Henry O. Havemeyer has paid $60,000 for two
portraits by Rembrandt of Nicolas Van Beeressteyn and his wife; and an extremely
large sum for the celebrated "Gilder" by the same artist. Mr. Henry G. Marquand has presented to the Metropolitan Museum of Art his collection of old
masters, the value of which is estimated at $250,000, the Van Dyck alone—a full-
length portrait—costing $25,000. At the famous Secretan sale in Paris on the
2d of July, 1889, De Hooghe's "Dutch Interior" was sold to an American for
$55,200, and Rubens's "David and Abigail" to another American for $22,400.
Several of the more important modern canvases at the same sale, on the 1st of
July, were secured by Americans also; but the celebrated "Angelus" of Millet
was finally knocked down to a representative of the French Government for
$110,600, after a spirited competition on the part of two American bidders, who
ceased their efforts only on learning that the representative of the French Government, M. Antonio Proust, was determined to get the picture, and had at his dis-

Louis Paul Dessar — A Shepherd at Étaples

posal the sum of $172,000 for the purpose. Loud cries of "*Vive la France!*" were heard in the auction-room when the Americans were defeated. It seems that M. Proust, who, as the Government's Special Commissioner for the Fine Arts at the

Universal Exhibition, had been brought into intimate relations with the French collectors, had made a special appeal to them not to allow the masterpiece of Millet
to go out of the country. These gentlemen responded by placing at his disposal
the $172,000 already mentioned; and M. Tirard, the President of the Council under
M. Carnot's administration, promised that they should be indemnified. But the
Government refused to ratify the purchase, and the "Angelus" then came into the
hands of Mr. Sutton, of the American Art Association. The largest sum hitherto paid
by an American for a French painting—or, indeed, for any painting, with the possible
exception of Rembrandt's "Gilder"—was the $60,000 of Mr. A. T. Stewart for
Meissonier's "1807," now in the Metropolitan Museum of Art; but there were two
American bids for the "Angelus" which exceeded $100,000 each. It is estimated
that there are at least $8,000,000 invested in the private art collections of the United
States. The most valuable of these collections is that of the late Mr. William H. Vanderbilt, which contains about two hundred pictures, worth more than $1,000,000.

Mr. Gari Melchers's first picture of importance was exhibited at the *Salon* of
1886, under the title of " Le Prêche" ("The Sermon"), a company of Protestant
peasants listening to an unseen preacher in a little church in Holland; and *L'Art*
did him the honor to reproduce two full-page studies made by him for the painting, together with a third study of smaller size. To the text which accompanied
these reproductions the artist contributed some autobiographical details. He was
born in 1860, in Detroit, Michigan, of German parents. His father was a sculptor
who had studied in Paris under Etex and Carpeaux, and who intended that his
son should enter the army or the navy. But the latter, even while a school-boy,
persuaded his parent to teach him drawing, and demonstrated his vocation for art.
At seventeen he left home for Europe, to continue his artistic education wherever
he should think best. Meeting another student, who was returning to Düsseldorf,
he contracted a friendship which led him also to that city, where he sojourned for
three years. In 1880 he went to Paris, entered the atelier of MM. Boulanger and
Lefebvre, and followed the academic course of the École des Beaux-Arts. Although
the funds allowed him by his father were by no means affluent, he succeeded in
visiting almost all the museums of Europe. In 1882 he sent to the *Salon* his first
contribution, a Breton interior, called " La Lettre." The next year his pictures
were " Pater Noster" and " A Woman of Attina, Italy "; and in 1885 he was
represented by the " Gueux de la Mer," two Dutch sailors at the capstan. Holland attracted him beyond all other countries, and he installed himself at Egmond-
aan-Zee, in a house which he and a brother artist (Mr. George Hitchcock) built
on the dunes. Winter and summer the two worked there; and the "Communion,"

which gained the Medal of Honor at the Paris Exposition of 1889, was painted
in a little Dutch Reformed church at Egmond, where the artist had often seen
the sacred ceremony performed. The clergyman in the picture is the minister of
that church, and all the communicants are worshipers there. For several weeks the
interior of the edifice was placed at Mr. Melchers's disposal, and he had no difficulty
in persuading the pious peasants to pose for him. M. Paul Leroi, in the same
number of *L'Art*, said, "This American artist is gifted with such sagacity of observa-

EUGÈNE A. LA CHAISE : *Souvenir of Japan.*

tion that the popular manners of the modern Netherlands will find very probably,
in this young man of twenty-six years, a painter as faithful as were the illustrious
contemporaries of Rembrandt." Mr. Melchers was "*un sincère*" of the school of
Thomas de Keyser, who painted portraits with such prodigious intensity of life,
and with a knowledge that defied all criticism. The "Sermon" was the work of
a painter of "high conscience," who did not believe that he had the right to
expose a painting unless he had studied it well. Firmness of drawing, knowledge
of composition, and ease of execution, distinguished the picture. This American

reproduced in full light—not with the somber eloquence of Josef Israels—the manners of the country of his artistic adoption as he daily observed them. He translated its character with the rarest sagacity, with an extraordinary intensity of assimilation, without excluding a certain amount of humor, but also without falling into that gangrene of *genre* painting, anecdote. "If the state," he added, "wished to enrich the Luxembourg Museum with true works of art, rather than yield to the influential and interested solicitations of one or another deputy or senator in favor of some dry fruit, it would acquire the 'Sermon' of Mr. Melchers and the 'In Arcady' of Mr. Alexander Harrison, and would receive the unanimous approbation of all those who, in the matter of painting, care for talent and not for intrigue." Since that time—now only three years—Mr. Melchers has received the first medal at Amsterdam, the first medal at Munich (equal to the Medal of Honor at the Paris *Salon*), a third-class medal and an Honorable Mention at the *Salon*, and the Medal of Honor at the Paris Exposition of 1889. That is to say, he has obtained more and greater recompenses for a man of his age than any other painter of modern times, possibly of any times. Detaille was thirty-two when he won his Medal of Honor; Melchers was only twenty-eight. His work is very little known in America, and our readers will be glad to see so large and admirable a reproduction of his masterpiece, the "Communion." The true spirit of devotion is seen in the faces of these humble communicants; religion with them is a vital force; they are sincere, unconscious, deeply moved. Hundreds of Madonnas in the Louvre seem affected and exaggerated by the side of these simple saints of contemporaneous life, whom Fra Angelico himself would admire. In this great picture Mr. Melchers has shown that a truly religious art is possible in this last agnostic quarter of the nineteenth century.

In connection with the reproduction of Mr. Robert J. Wickenden's "Approach of Evening," I have received a biographical sketch prepared by a friend of the artist, which deserves to be given in full because of its representative character, not less than its intrinsic interest: Mr. Wickenden was born in the classic old city of Rochester, England, on the 8th of July, 1861. His father, a sea-captain, had been lost some six months previously, leaving the widowed mother with three sons. His brothers, Thomas and James, older by some eight and ten years respectively, came to America in early manhood, and Robert followed them with his mother in 1873, to Toledo, Ohio, where he spent several years. Having always shown a decided tendency toward art, he commenced to study definitely, getting such advice as was possible from local artists, and working carefully from Nature. Going afterward to New York, during the seasons of 1880–'81 and 1881–'82, he studied

ELLEN K. BAKER : *Tranquillity*.

at the Art Students' League, under J. Carroll Beckwith and William M. Chase, returning in the intervals to Detroit, where for two seasons he set up his studio and gained a certain local reputation. Early in 1883 he went to Paris, and after a short period of study at the Academy Colarrossi, under Courtois and Collin, he entered the École des Beaux-Arts, in the atelier of Ernest Hébert, now Director of the French Academy at Rome. For two seasons he took advantage of the strong academic influences of this world-famed school. But much time was also given to the study of the riches of art of all ages so profusely gathered at Paris. Greek sculpture, and the Italian and Flemish masters, especially pleased him, and he spent much time in absorbing their spirit and analyzing their methods. Among the moderns, Millet, Corot, Daubigny, and Rousseau held him with great charm, and, both in the old and the new, it was his effort to find that subtle essence of beauty, the same in all ages, though appearing under diverse forms. The summer of 1883, spent partly by the bedside of a sick friend, was finished at Brolles, some miles across the Forest of Fontainebleau from Barbizon, whither he often walked to see the houses and surroundings of the painters whose art he so much loved. This was a season of close work, filling commissions received from America and painting a forest interior, "La Glaneuse en Forêt," exhibited at the *Salon* of 1884, and afterward with another picture, "Novembre," at the Inaugural Exhibition of the American Art Association at New York. In July of this year he went to Jersey to paint some cattle and pastoral subjects for which he held commissions, and which occupied him the better part of a year, broken by occasional visits to London and Paris. At the Dudley Gallery, in 1885, he exhibited "A Sunny Morning near Beaumont, Jersey." Coming to America in the autumn of this year, he took a studio in the Sherwood Building, New York, and sent to the autumn Academy "A Jersey Milkmaid "—a fresh figure clad in light tints is coming down a woodland path, carrying two of the quaint brass cans peculiar to Jersey. At the Water-Color Exhibition of 1886 he was represented by three other works, and, at the spring Academy, by "Driving Home the Turkeys" and "A Spring-time Idyl." Returning to Europe in the summer of 1886, he exhibited at the French Gallery, Pall Mall, London, "When the Kye come Home," a Jersey moon-rise, which introduced the artist to several London dealers, among them Mr. Martin Colnaghi, of the Haymarket. After an interruption caused by illness, he completed the large picture, "An Arcadian Shepherdess," exhibited by the American Art Association in 1887: A shepherdess clad in light Greek drapery is reposing under a giant oak at the hour of twilight; as she plays upon her lyre, some sheep gather sleepily around, while others browse in the meadow beyond, watched by the faithful dog, and across the misty valley rises the faint full moon. The whole intention was to portray the peace and beauty of pastoral life. At the *Salon* of 1888 he exhibited "A Spinner" and "Souvenir d'Automne," the former an old peasant-woman spinning by a bright fire, over which is a pot of steaming *bouillon;* the latter a group of autumn fruits and flowers. A member of the Paris-American Committee for the Munich International Exposition, he sent a study of "Oaks, Isle of Jersey"; and to the "Exposition International du Blanc et Noir," at Paris, the same year, some seven water-color studies. At the Universal Exposition of 1889, in Paris, he exhibited "Noon," a hay-field study with a scythe thrown down in the foreground; and a water-color, "Côtes Fleuries, Jersey." His *Salon* picture for 1889, herewith reproduced, "The Approach of Evening," was painted at Auvers-sur-Oise, where the artist has spent several summers, in the country so much loved by Daubigny and Corot, occupying for a time the old studio of the former master. Amid these surroundings he saw and painted the subject given, which the following lines, written by himself at the same time, explain:

THEODORE ROBINSON : *Watching the Cow*

"The grain that is ready to fall,
    The day that is ready to die,
The valley that soon must be passed,
    And the Cross lifted ever on high.

> " Let me patiently wait by the Cross,
> The end of my journey is near ;
> Though night with its darkness surround,
> God is nigh—no evil I fear "—

thus expressing the patient faith of the old peasant, "*Attendant le bon Dieu*"— as some rustics, who were returning from the fields at the time, put it. Most of Mr. Wickenden's pictures have gone directly to those who commissioned them, without being exhibited ; but, feeling the need of a broader recognition, he will henceforward endeavor to frequent the exhibitions with examples of his art. The painter of the " Brittany Girl," Mr. Edward Henry Potthast, is a native of Cincinnati, and a pupil of M. Cormon, of Paris. At the *Salon* his picture was catalogued under the name " Une Bretonne."

Mr. Frederick A. Bridgman's contributions to the Universal Exposition at Paris in 1889 were six in number. " The Pirate of Love " told an Algerian story in three panels. The first panel introduced us to a lovely woman sitting on a balcony, the second showed her fainting in the arms of a vicious brigand, and in the third she lay wounded and dead on the floor. Another canvas portrayed the " Fête of the Prophet," with women wholly or partly veiled or unveiled. In the " Negro Fête at Blidah " were seen the wild dances of some Africans. The " Horse-Market at Cairo" showed some animals as graceful as those of Fromentin. " On the House-Tops, Algiers," were figures in white leaning over the parapets ; and the " Portrait of Mme. B." afforded a well-used opportunity for gifts that are by no means usual. While these pictures were speaking for his versatility and power, the artist was finishing in his studio another one of great beauty, which appears in this Portfolio, under the title of " Souvenir of Tlemcen." This handsome Arabian of northern Africa wears a small bodice over an under-garment with long sleeves of lace caught up at the shoulder. A *foutah*, or scarf, of light-blue striped silk, is tied about her waist, and on her head is thrown another *foutah* of dark-blue cotton, with stripes of golden thread, which takes the place of the large white *haik* worn in the streets. She wears also a conical cap of red velvet embroidered in gold, and a necklace of gold coins. Beside her, near the chrysanthemums that she is watering, is an earthen jar shaped like a fish ; but her eyes are occupied with matters entirely foreign to those that engage her hands. As Byron might have said :

> " Round her she made an atmosphere of life,
> The very air seemed lighter from her eyes,
> They were so soft and beautiful, and rife
> With all we can imagine from the skies ;

Her eyelashes, though dark as night, were tinged
(It is the country's custom), but in vain;
For those large black eyes were so blackly fringed,
The glossy rebels mocked the jetty stain,
And in their native beauty stood avenged."

The young painter of the "Sunday at Étaples," Mr. Louis Paul Dessar, studied under Mr. William E. Plimpton in New York city, and also under Professor Will-

GEORGE W. COHEN : *The Reading.*

marth, of the National Academy of Design.   On arriving in Paris in 1886 he chose M. Bouguereau and M. Tony Robert Fleury as his masters, and he has exhibited already twice at the *Salon*.   His picture of the grandmother reading from the Bible to her granddaughter is a piece of sweet and honest sentiment, and suggests Goethe's famous observation that life resides wholly in the eternal feminine.

The principal facts of Miss Elizabeth Gardner's life are well known, and have already been mentioned in an earlier part of this work.   This successful artist enjoys the distinction of being the only American woman who has won a medal at the *Salon*.

She went to Paris from her home at Exeter, New Hampshire, after graduation at
the seminary in Auburndale, Massachusetts, and has lived in the French capital ever
since 1867. Her professional association has been with the modern French masters
of the classic school, with men who value drawing and whose aim is serious. Her
figures belong to the same category that Cabanel and Bouguereau have rendered
illustrious. They are sculpturesque—"Cornelia," "Ruth and Naomi," "Moses,"
"Priscilla," "Daphnis and Chloe," "Corinne," and "Maud Muller." More recently
she has treated *genre* subjects, but these also, like the "Too Imprudent," have a
classic air. This brilliant young American has the severe tastes of the direction
of the École des Beaux-Arts. Did the awarders of her recompenses at the *Salon*

LEE LASH   *Old Sailors in a Retreat.*

mean to recognize the fact that there was at least one American woman who
knew how to draw, and who could discern the difference between the beautiful
and the pettily pretty?

Mr. La Chaise's "Souvenir of Japan" shows some of the results of two years'
study in that interesting country. The woman is dancing gracefully and with
some vigor in a hall overlooking the sea, accompanied by an instrumentalist who
can easily be counted among her admirers. Her black-velvet gown, handsomely
embroidered in colors and gold, partly conceals her scarlet skirt, her hair is profusely ornamented with handsome pins, and in her right hand she holds a scarlet
fan. A certain facility in the use of her wrists reminds one of the dancing-girls

of Java, who created a sensation in the "Village Javanais" on the Esplanade des Invalides, in Paris, in the summer of 1889.

Before hanging the pictures in the American section of the Universal Exposition of 1889, the jury voted that the place of honor should be occupied by Mr. W. T. Dannat's "Quartette," which had great success at the *Salon* of 1884, and was proposed for a First-Class Medal. But the refusal of Congress to remove the high tariff on works of art produced an unfavorable prejudice in the minds of Frenchmen; and when the painting was sent to the Universal Exposition, M. Proust, the

CARLE J. BLENNER : *Country Life.*

Special Commissioner of the Fine Arts, together with other distinguished men, endeavored, it is said, to dissuade Mr. Dannat from serving on the International Jury of Recompense, because the members of that jury could not compete for prizes. Had the artist yielded to their wishes, he might have received a Medal of Honor at the Exposition; but he chose to sacrifice his own interests, and was elected secretary of the jury, which was composed of forty-one members, about one half of them distinguished French artists, the rest being foreigners. The four figures that appear in the "Quartette" are types to be found in Alcazar, in the north of Spain, where Mr. Dannat studied them. They are very·remarkable for vitality and personal force, especially the handsome woman dressed in black, with narrow scarlet ribbons, who plays the castanets, and who is worthy to have been described in the annals of Cervantes. The "Quartette" was exhibited for some months at the Metropolitan Museum of Art in New York, of which city Mr. Dannat is a native. He has already received a medal of the third class at the *Salon*, and his rank as a colorist is high. The "Blonde Profile," sometimes called "A Study in Red," is extremely graceful in pose.

Miss Ellen K. Baker, the painter of the "Tranquillity," went to Paris eleven years ago and studied art under M. Paul Soyer. She first exhibited in the *Salon* of 1879, and has been represented annually in that institution, except when absent in America. Her work has been hung in all the large cities of the United States, and has a permanent place in the Museum of Detroit and the Art Gallery of Buffalo, besides being known in England and in Bavaria. Though fond of painting children, and very successful in portraiture, she has handled also many *genre* subjects, of which the "Tranquillity" is a representative at once adequate and pleasing. It deals with types of Picardy, where the artist is accustomed to spend her summers, and it tells its simple story with naturalness, ease, and grace. Miss Baker is a native of Fairfield, Herkimer County, New York. Her home in France is on the Seine, overlooking the city of Paris, in a picturesque neighborhood, where many of the people continue to wear the caps and costumes of the provinces from which they came.

In the "Portrait of Mme. P." Mr. Charles Sprague Pearce illustrates Delacroix's principle in drawing, that "form without movement is nothing." The figure seems to be stepping out of the canvas from a greenish-gray background, while at the same time the sense of repose is perfect. No labored details of the steel-blue costume, or palm-leaf fan, or white dog, detract from the effect of the facial expression. The immaterial is not sacrificed to the material. There is something more than correctness of linear design. Grace, elegance, seductiveness, a capacity for performing a special ministry—"the good stars met in her horoscope and made her of spirit, fire, and dew"—surely such traits in portraiture are not so common nowadays as to cause weariness.

Mr. Theodore Robinson's idyl appeared in the *Salon* under the name "Vachère"— a woman who watches the cows when they are pasturing. We have no corresponding word for it in English, because the occupation which it describes does not regularly exist in America as it does in France. The artist has not chosen an ugly model, as do many young American painters of the French peasantry. In fact, his figure is precisely the reverse, as might have been expected of a pupil of Carolus-Duran and Gérôme.

The bride in Mr. E. L. Weeks's "Hindoo Marriage" is on her way to the house of the groom, who does not appear in this part of the ceremony. She is of high caste, and the carriage in which she rides has a gold-embroidered dome, scarlet curtains with silk fringes, and breaks of large copper tubes partly protected by painted leather, and is drawn by a pair of oxen with large humps, enormous

ARTHUR F. MATHEWS : A Study in Holland

horns, long pendent ears, and silver head-trappings. Brahmans, of distinguished
social position, beat tom-toms as the procession of *Nautch* dancing-girls advances
from under a dark arch in a street of an East Indian city, where the houses of
carved teak-wood have brilliant colors, time-worn, and washed every morning.
The tones of the old carved brick walls are gray in some places and tawny in
others. Mr. Weeks made his studies for the picture in the street which he has
depicted, and the carriage was loaned to him for the purpose by a young Hindoo,
who owned several equipages that were let for such ceremonies. Two of the
Brahmans are portraits. The foremost one wears a white tunic and lilac turban.
The composition was painted expressly for the Universal Exposition of 1889 in
Paris, where it gained a First Medal for the artist, and was greatly admired by
thousands of visitors, both for the literary interest of its subject and the beauty
of its art.

Mr. George W. Cohen, the author of "The Reading," was born in New York
city, on the 4th of August, 1861. He began his studies at Munich, under Prof.
Loeftz, in the spring of 1884, and won a bronze medal the next year at the
Royal Academy of that city. In 1888 he went to Paris and continued his novitiate
under Lefebvre, Boulanger, Constant, and Doucet, in the Académie Julien. "The
Reading" is his first picture at the *Salon.*

Mr. Frank M. Boggs's picture, the "Place de la Bastille," reproduces, under
decidedly pictorial conditions, one of the best-known quarters of Paris, formerly the
site of the celebrated castle where prisoners of state were confined and often tortured.
The lofty bronze monument, one hundred and fifty-four feet high, in the center
of the picture, is called the "Column of July," after the Revolution of July, 1830.
It bears the inscription, "À la gloire des citoyens français qui s'armèrent et com-
battirent pour la défense des libertés publiques dans les mémorables journées des
27, 28, et 29 juillet, 1830." The column is surmounted by a golden figure of
the Genius of Liberty. Mr. Boggs had the honor of seeing his picture purchased
by the French Government.

Mr. Lee Lash is of Austrian parentage, although at the time of his birth in
Victoria, Vancouver's Island, his parents were citizens of the United States. When
an infant he was taken to San Francisco, and that city has since been his home.
He went to Paris in 1880 and studied under Boulanger and Lefebvre. His present
ambition is to paint athletic subjects in San Francisco. Mr. Lash is a man of very
decided views on art-matters. "I don't see," he remarks, "why we should not
make our pictures talk as the pen talks; and why, when an artist paints some
figures in the picturesque Breton costume, he should not so paint them as to have

a tendency to prevent Paris bonnets from going down to Brittany, as they have
already gone into the environs of the city.   Nothing is slower in progress than
art, because we have contented ourselves with doing what our predecessors have
done.   An athlete should be painted so that every young man who sees him will
envy him, will appreciate the beauty and value of a well-developed body.   But
when we look at a picture to-day we contemplate it chiefly as a piece of technique; we speak of the air that is in it, of the tone, of the textures; we don't

SIMON H. VEDDER : *Sunshine in a Cavern.*

feel the sentiment of the work, as a pious worshiper does that of a beautiful Ma-
donna.   I once painted a subject called 'Absinthe,' designed to show the evils of
intemperance.   A celebrated French artist to whom I showed it said: 'Leave ideas
for literary men; we painters want grace and elegance.'   You don't stop at the
technique in Millet's pictures; you feel the peasant's soul. . . . In my picture of
'Old Sailors,' I confess that the subject has not a great deal of importance.   It is
an old sailors' home, and probably shows the public that these old chaps after a

life of hardships have been received into a sanctuary that is a proof of the benevo-
lence of mankind. This is good enough as far as it goes, but the aim might have
been higher. A French critic, however, pleased me by writing that I had painted
a lot of old salts in a *bourgeois* costume and yet had made them look like old salts,
even without their sea-dress. He had just seen a picture of some journalists at dinner,
who, if in sailors' costume, would look like sailors! In other words, he felt that
I had got the soul of the thing. If I thought that there was no more in art than
mere execution, I should lack stimulus."

Mr. Carle J. Blenner began his art studies at New Haven, Connecticut, in the
Yale School of Fine Arts. He is a pupil in Paris of Bouguereau and Tony R.
Fleury, and has also been instructed by Schenck at Écouen. His works have
appeared at the London Academy, the Munich International Exhibition, and the
Salons of 1888 and 1889. Mr. Arthur F. Mathews was born in California, October
1, 1859, and, after studying architecture in his father's office, and gaining the first
prize offered by the *Sanitary Engineer* for the best plan for a model school-house,
determined to devote himself to painting, and soon entered his name at the Académie
Julien, where Boulanger and Lefebvre were his preceptors, and where he gained
prizes for painting, drawing, and composition. The piquant "Study in Holland"
represents his favorite model in an every-day performance. Mr. S. H. Vedder's
"Sunshine in a Cavern" is a chapter from the prehistoric ages. The savage young
cave-dweller amuses himself by playing the pipe to a pair of cubs who, having
been captured by some hunters, are in process of domestication as pets. He seems
to be teaching them to dance to his music. The skin on which he sits belongs to
an animal of the hyena species, and the dish out of which one of the bears is drinking is of yellow clay. Mr. Vedder studied art two seasons in the schools of the
Metropolitan Museum in New York city, and afterward in Paris under Gérôme, Bouguereau, and Tony R. Fleury. He is a native of Montgomery County, New York,
and was born October 9, 1866. Mr. Ernest L. Major, the painter of the "Young
Knitter," was born in Washington, D. C., April 26, 1864. He took a gold medal
for drawing at the public school, and his father intended that he should learn
engraving. For this purpose he determined to make a thorough study of drawing,
and went to the Art Students' League, New York, for two seasons, where Messrs.
Chase and Dewing were his instructors. He was compelled to return to Washington, but succeeded in getting to New York again with his own funds, and com-
peted successfully for the Harper-Hallgarten Scholarship at the League (described in
an earlier part of this portfolio), which gave him the means of study in Europe for
three years. He began exhibiting at the *Salon* in 1886. The "Young Knitter"

ERNEST L. MAJOR : A Young Knitter.

lives in Picardy, at Étaples.   Mr. Peter Alfred Gross, the painter of "The Wooden
Bridge," in the Haute-Saône, France, was born on a farm near Allentown, Pennsylvania.   He has worked in a saw-mill, has taught school, has made pen-and-ink
sketches for the lithographers, has published lithographed show-cards and bird's-eye

views of various cities. He began to paint in
1882, under the noted landscapist, M. Edmond
Yvon, and sent his first picture to the *Salon* the
next year. For the last three years he has been
a pupil of Edmond Petitjean. His energy and
talents are of a high order.

Mr. Carl Gutherz's genius has produced the
"Borne away by Angels," an imaginative composition of decided beauty. Its title in the *Salon*
was "Arcessita ab Angelis." Death appears, not
as the grinning skeleton of the middle ages, but
as a gracious friend. His gray robes, floating
beneath the body of the woman, symbolize ashes.
All Mr. Gutherz's works abound in poetry,
even *genre* subjects, like "The Useful and the
Ornamental"—a *bourgeois* wife with a pot of
flowers in one hand and a basket of vegetables
in the other.

The "Charlotte Corday" of Mr. Julian Story was suggested by Lamartine's
well-known description : "They tied her hands and folded back her robe from
her shoulders. 'A toilet of death,' she exclaimed, 'made by hands somewhat rude,
but leading to immortality.'" This courageous woman was beautiful as well, and
Mr. Story has depicted both her beauty and her courage.

PETER A. GROSS : *The Wooden Bridge.*

IDA WAUGH : *Hagar and Ishmael*

VIII.

E. I. COUSE : *The Wayside Shrine.*

NEVER before did American art assert itself so strongly and present itself so pleasingly as at the Paris Exposition of 1889. Its triumphs were the amazement of foreigners and the pride of Americans. A discriminating writer in *L'Art* had indeed complained, three years earlier, that at the *Salon* Melchers, Alexander Harrison, and Walter MacEwen, all hailing from the United States, were stronger than most of the French painters to whom recompenses had been awarded. But so conservative a journal as Mr. Hamerton's *Portfolio* declared, in its regular review of that great Exposition, that the American contribution was a marvel of evolution since

of vision, and in the dexterity of hand and general accomplishment, which it is the
gift of the French to teach.   Scarcely in the whole show was there "a contrast
so violent as that between the American and English sections.   It was stronger
than that between the English and French sections; stronger even than that

CHARLES THÉRIAT : *A Corner in Biskra (Algeria)*.

between the English and the Spanish or Italian rooms." Perhaps no praise more
grateful was ever received by the men who have produced those recent ideals of
American art which it has been the duty and the pleasure of this book to reproduce.   Opinion in their own country has long been opposed to that of Mr.
Hamerton's *Portfolio* on this subject.   The very month that this tribute of the

leading English art review appeared, the readers of a New York journal were told
that it would be pleasant to feel sure that American art as a whole was beginning
to take on some sort of national complexion : "It is well for a nation to have
an art of its own. The best art is, it may be said, cosmopolitan, and this may

CLIFFORD GRAYSON · *Morning*

be so; but the individuality of a nation ought to find artistic expression as well
as the individuality of a person.   America is assuredly *sui generis;* yet one can
not truthfully assert the same of much that it produces in the way of art.   Its
humorous literature is of the soil, and so is some of its poetry.   Some of its fiction
is genuinely American, though its music is not, and its pictures are not.   Its chief
painters are artistically the children of other lands; they go abroad to study, and
stay there to paint.   The subjects they choose are rarely American; they take little
pains to reproduce American landscapes or types of character; they pay little atten-

SUSAN STOUPE : *The Lake.*

tion to American historical episodes.   They are Parisian, rather than New-Yorkian."
In the same spirit one of the best-known American men of letters has criticised
these volumes of RECENT IDEALS OF AMERICAN ART, because, though "a beautiful
and magnificent tribute to the artistic genius of the United States," they contain
some pictures by Americans who reside in Paris, and who paint subjects not
American.   The scheme of this book, it may frankly be confessed, was not laid
within lines so restricted.   Artists of the West, the South, the East, and the North
are represented in it, whether their work was done in the United States, in England,

FRANK H. RICHARDSON : *Springtime at Giret, France.*

in Germany, Italy, or France. The American spirit, wherever its activities are displayed, is still American; and the American artist, whether painting in San Francisco or in Munich, in New York or in Paris, in Boston or in Rome, displays— and must display—the American spirit in his work. It is this fact that explains "the miracle of evolution" which struck so forcibly the writer in Mr. Hamerton's *Portfolio.* If the American painter shows traces of his French education, it is because, while remaining an American, he has acquired the results of the best teaching possible in art, namely, "directness of vision, dexterity of hand, and general accomplishment"; and it is entirely true that English painting, as a rule, is inferior in these respects to American or French painting. Most friends of American painting will hope that American painters will continue to study in France until America can as well teach them what France is now teaching them. No intelligent visitor to the late Paris Exposition can doubt that its American pictures showed really and conclusively the effects of that teaching which the

English critic has enumerated; nor can he doubt that, whatever the subject chosen by an American painter—be it a Seine landscape, a Munich street-scene, an English interior, an Italian orange-girl, or a view in Central Park—the American spirit can make itself felt in the treatment of it. For the American sees his subject with the eyes of an American.

WINSARETTY SINGER : *A Portrait.*

The only American who makes a practice of painting life in the cities—in the parks, in the streets, and on the house-tops—is Mr. Childe Hassam. Sometimes he reproduces the flower-gardens of country-houses, where the women are so charming, and, above all, so "paintable"; but it is in the cities that he chiefly finds his subjects, where the women in out-door costumes are not less charming, and where the correlated atmospheric effects appeal to the artist's pencil. Mr. Hassam's pictures tell interesting stories and at the same time record the most delicate play of light and shade. They belong to a class that loses something by being photographed. The "Twilight in Paris" is a house-top arranged with a bench and with pots of flowers and shrubs, as the Parisians are so fond of doing in the spring. The picture was painted on just such an elevation on the heights of Montmartre, in the northern part of the city, under the influence of a delicate and clear twilight softened by the tender haze that hangs over the capital at that hour. The two girls in white gowns, the azalias and hydrangeas, and the terra-cotta

WILLIAM BAIRD : *A Shady Nook.*

chimney-pots, whose tints vary according to their age, are bathed in the last warm rays of the sun. Mr. Hassam evidently felt, as he has certainly expressed, the poetry of Wordsworth's "rich and balmy eve" under the conditions of Parisian spring-time.

Miss Anna Elizabeth Klumpke was born in San Francisco in 1856, and went to school in Cannstadt, near Stuttgart, Germany, in 1871. Nine years later she began her art studies in Julian's Academy, Paris, under MM. Tony Robert Fleury, Bouguereau, and De Vuillefroy, where she received a silver medal for drawing and a first grand prize at the annual *concours de portrait* between the men and women pupils. In 1885 she won an Honorable Mention at the *Salon*, and in 1889 a third-class medal at the Universal Exposition, and the Temple Gold Medal at the Philadelphia Exhibition. Among her best portraits is that of her mother, which appears in this work, and was highly praised at the *Salon* of 1889 by both French and American critics. Her *genre* picture, "Une Merveilleuse," in the time of the Directory, was exhibited in New York city. Miss Klumpke and Miss Elizabeth Gardner are the most successful of the American women who paint in Paris. The "Portrait of my Mother" has remarkable directness of vision and other masterly qualities.

Hagar, bending in anguish and amazement over the body of Ishmael, who lies on his back in the hot sand, is the dramatic motive of Miss Ida Waugh. The young girl, kneeling at an old "Wayside Shrine" in Brittany, is an American whom Mr. Eanger I. Couse has clothed in the costume of the last century, and whose spirit of devotion is expressed by attitude alone, her face not being visible. A crescent-moon is rising over the hills in the evening twilight. Most of Mr. Couse's subjects are elfish, as in the beautiful "Dream of the Fairies," where a

THOMAS HOVENDEN : *The Pride of the Family.*

troop of romantic little creatures with musical instruments are visiting a child, who, after reading a book of fairy-tales, has fallen asleep on a terrace. This picture will be sent to the Paris *Salon* of 1890. The artist, a native of East Saginaw, Michigan, made money enough by fresco-painting to spend two years, and take several prizes, at the schools of the New York Academy of Design. Then, by teaching and by painting portraits, he earned enough more to pay his expenses to Paris, and pursue his studies at the École des Beaux-Arts and at Julian's Academy, where, at the end of a year, he was awarded a prize for a

WILLIAM T. TRIGO : *The Guard of the Flag.*

drawing from life. He first exhibited at the Academy of Design in New York in 1884, and since 1888 has been represented at the *Salon*. The "Corner in Biskra" is due to the travels in Algeria of Mr. Charles Theriat, a native of New York, who went to Europe in 1872, in his twelfth year, and has had a studio in Paris since 1880. For four years he was a student in Julian's atelier. In 1887 his health rendered it impossible for him to spend his winters in Paris, and he has recently lived at least half of every year in the south of France or in Algeria, sometimes going as far as Touggurth, Ouargla, and El-Oued. The "Corner in Biskra" is rather a study than a picture: the corner, the man, and the pots were to be seen daily in Biskra in the spring of 1888, and are perhaps there now. Mr. Theriat has much of the modern artist's love of the "plein air"; out-doors, particularly in full sunshine, profoundly stirs his emotions, though his works do not show so fundamental a change as do those of M. Roll since the painting of that distinguished French artist's "L'Inondation," with its grewsome spots and clayey tints.

ANNA E. KLUMPKE : *Portrait of my Mother.*

Ten years ago, when finishing the text of "American Painters," I wrote that at least some earnest men and women were hopefully waiting for a new revelation of the beautiful in Nature. To-day I can not but feel that in many of the pictures reproduced in these volumes may really be recognized a new "revelation of the beautiful in Nature." The causes that have produced this auspicious result I have endeavored to depict in these pages; and I venture to express the belief that the strong and special charm of simplicity of purpose, the honesty not warped by the supposed demands of a vitiated public taste, the personal and intimate sentiment of the real, and the love of perfection in workmanship, which now characterize the representative American artist, have a profound and perfect value in the ennobling influence which his art is exerting upon our social life.

FREDERIC WAUGH : *Sympathy.*

ARTHUR QUARTLEY : *Sunset.*

SUPPLEMENT

MR. Clifford Grayson has expressed the idea of "Mourning" in his picture of the old woman in black cloak and gown, and white cap, leaning upon her staff in a French cemetery, where are buried those whose departure has left her desolate. Her thoughts are chiefly concerned with the occupant of the grave above which rises a simple cross of wood, on which hangs a wreath of immortelles. A young poplar towers near the gray stone wall behind her—emblem, perchance, of the youth whose beauty and vigor were her pride. This canvas was hung at the Paris *Salon* of 1889. Miss Susan Sroufe deals with a peaceful landscape effect, in which a boat-house, an antiquated wharf, and a boatman just starting out upon the placid surface of the lake, are the principal features. She does not miss the point, nor does she slight any part of the rational basis of her pictorial scheme. After a business career as civil engineer and banker, Mr. F. H. Richardson went across the Atlantic and enrolled his name at Julian's Academy in Paris. He had already given many stray moments to art, but his first serious study was in that institution, under M. Boulanger and M. Ducet. He is a member of the Paint and Clay Club of Boston, and an exhibitor in Munich and at the *Salon*. His "Spring-time at Grez, France," was painted in that charming village, on the edge of the Forest of Fontainebleau. During the last two summers he has made many sketches at Concarneau, on the coast of Brittany. The sanity of his interpretations of

Nature is the most striking of their qualities.   Mr. Frederick Waugh's very pleasing composition, "Sympathy," is admirably described by its title.   Mr. Henry
Bacon has made many studies of bandit-life in the Island of Corsica, and these
studies have led him, he says, to a clear apprehension of the fundamental traits of
the First Napoleon.   The portrait of the lady standing in a doorway, her face and
the Normandy landscape behind her brightly lighted, was in the *Salon* of 1886.
Miss Winnaretta Singer, the artist, is a daughter of the late Isaac M. Singer, and
a native of Yonkers, New York.   She was educated in England, and has studied
art for four years in Paris, in the Barrias atelier.   Miss Sroufe, on the other hand,
was born in Petaluma, California, and has been a resident of San Francisco since
her early childhood, with the exception of three years of study in Paris under
Edmond Yon and François Flameng.   In the case of neither of these ladies does
art seem to be a joyless struggle with difficulties.

Mr. William Baird began his professional life in 1866, in Chicago, as a draughtsman for wood-engravers, and studied painting at the same time.   Two public-
spirited citizens of that Northwestern metropolis—Mr. W. B. Howard and General
Corse—saw some of his work, were pleased with it, and testified their pleasure
by proposing to provide Mr. Baird with funds for three years' study of art in
Paris.   The young artist accepted the generous offer, and placed himself under
the care of the painter Yvon.   His home has been in the French capital ever
since, with the exception of a sojourn in Brittany during the Franco-German War.
He received a silver medal at Versailles, a bronze medal at Cherbourg, and a third-
class medal at the Nice International Exhibition.   The title of his picture, "A
Shady Nook," expresses its motive; the artist speaks in the tones of actual life,
but without undue familiarity.

Mr. Thomas Hovenden's "Pride of the Family" is American in subject, in the
sense of presenting a scene of American life; and its technical merits are of a
high order.   This painter is a native of Cork, Ireland, who came to the United
States in 1863, in his twenty-third year, after a course of study in the South Kensington Museum.   Eleven years subsequently he went to Paris and became a pupil
of Cabanel.   To the *Salon* of 1876 he sent his "Image-Seller," now owned by
Mr. William T. Evans, and well known to the readers of this book.   In 1878 he
sent an episode of the war in La Vendée, which on another occasion I described
as follows: An old peasant is sharpening a sword for a young volunteer who is
about to start on an expedition.   He glances along the edge of the blade and
tests its sharpness, while the youthful soldier, his son and the father of two fine
children, waits in full uniform to receive it.   At his feet lies his powder-horn;

in a great chair in the corner, near a tall dresser, is his musket; by his side hangs his scabbard. In front of the fireplace the grandmother and one of the children are molding bullets over the charcoal burning in a brazier. All the accessories serve admirably to complete the story. The soldier's wife, her arms thrown protectingly over the cradle in which her infant sleeps, is of Spartan temper. She wishes the sword to be sharp, and she wishes her husband to use it; yet in her face are reflected emotions most pitiful. Mr. Hovenden has told with the same successful cleverness his story of the vain young negro-woman, who is the " Pride of the Family," and his technique has improved. It was once asked of him, after his return from Paris, whether he would be able to use his professional acquisitions in the service of creations of his own; or whether, like so many of his comrades who had enjoyed similar advantages, he would fail to display a crea- tive spirit when starting out for himself in the midst of American surroundings. Before he had been in this country two years, it was said of him: " He has shown himself capable of independent poetic expression. He has grown since he left his master. He has done enough to satisfy his friends that he is an artist.

HENRY BACON : A Corsican Bandit.

He manifests the power of awakening sentiment." Certainly, nothing less than this can be said of Mr. Hovenden to-day. The "Pride of the Family" is worthy of a place beside the best efforts of Winslow Homer.

The "Asylum" of Mr. Walter Gay represents a home for old women in one of the provinces of France, and is painted in a delicate tone, the fine and broad treatment of the light constituting its special charm. The young woman in the background is a speaking contrast.

Mr. William H. Howe, author of the " In Normandy," enjoys the reputation of being the most vigorous of the Paris-Americans who paint cattle. The press of that city has spoken of him as " an American who is inspired by Troyon," and as a man whose work "does not disavow Paul Potter." He won a gold medal at the *Salon* of 1888, and another at the Paris Universal Exposition of 1889. He admires most of the work of Troyon, and thinks that the latter's only defect is in his drawing. " If Troyon," he says, " had the drawing of Van Marcke, he would be perfect. But Van Marcke's pictures have no tones." One of Mr. Howe's most characteristic works is his contribution to the *Salon* of 1888, the "Early Start to Market," representing a Dutch peasant driving four cattle to Amsterdam over a long stretch of lowlands, with the Zuyder Zee in the distance, and the general effect of an early wet morning in Holland. Mr. Howe has spent many pleasant days in those regions with that great and lamented young Dutchman, Mauve. One of his earliest and most generous patrons is Mr. Catlin, of St. Louis.

Mr. William T. Trego is of artistic lineage, his father, Mr. J. K. Trego, being an esteemed portrait and animal painter of Philadelphia, and his uncle an artist of recognized ability. He took the first prize at the Academy of Fine Arts in that city, under the instruction of Professor Thomas Eakins, for his picture of the " Battery en Route," which was bought by Mr. Fairman Rogers and given to that institution, where it now hangs in the permanent collection of art-works. Two years later, in 1884, Mr. A. M. Zane, of Philadelphia, bought his canvas entitled " Washington's March to Valley Forge, 1777." " The Pursuit," another military picture, is owned by Mr. Jerome B. Wheeler, of New York ; the " Battery Halt," by the American Art Association ; and the " Passing Charge " and "A Charge at Fair Oaks," by Mr. Thomas B. Clarke. " The Guard of the Flag," reproduced in this portfolio, is Mr. Trego's first contribution to the *Salon*, and the subject was chosen out of compliment to the warm personal friends he has made in France, particularly to his favorite masters, M. Bouguereau and M. Robert-Fleury.

The two most representative works of Mr. Charles S. Reinhart are the "Washed Ashore " and " Awaiting the Absent," which established and promulgated his repu-

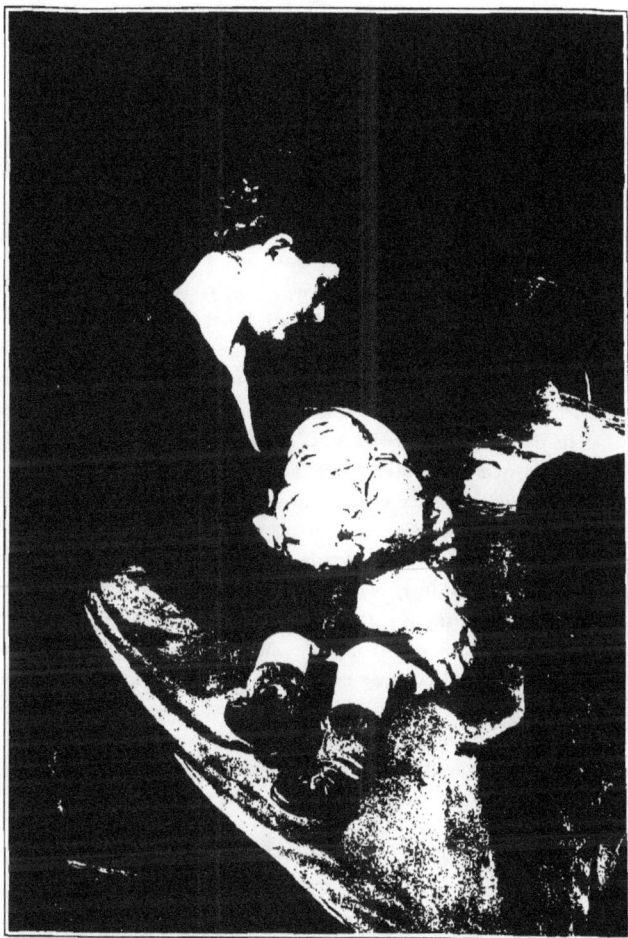

ELIZABETH NOURSE — *J. M. 89.*

tation at the Paris Universal Exposition of 1889. The latter picture discloses a
not unusual scene on the coast of Normandy—sailors' wives, mothers, and friends
watching their vessel in a storm; the former picture—a sequel to the other
discloses a dead body washed ashore. A more dramatic conception has seldom

been portrayed by an artist's pencil; and if, without violating a confidence, I might be permitted to quote from a letter written by the painter to a friend who had asked for some details regarding the subject, I should cite these words: "The man kneeling is making the sign of the cross—praying for the soul of the dead, whom he knows not, but who is one of his *métier*, who has run the same dangers, and whose end may be his. This is the key-note to the picture—the touch of brotherly love, the sympathy born of common destiny. It is the life of the common people of the coast, the drama of the sea that repeats itself year after year, as long as its breakers beat against the rocks and the poor fishermen go down into the sea in ships. I have told my story simply, as Nature tells it, without melodrama. I have exposed the corpse frankly before the spectator just as I saw it, without any subterfuge or trick whatsoever. Some tender souls may be shocked, but who has not a profound impression in the presence of Death?" The circumstances under which the painter conceived his subject are said to have been as follows: "In the midst of a terrific gale, and surrounded by a crowd of shrieking and praying women, Reinhart stood helpless while eight fishing-boats went ashore on the rocks, their spars snapping like matches, and the sailors clinging to the broken and tangled cordage only to be overcome at last by the relentless breakers. Some got safely to shore, but the entire crew of one boat (from Dieppe) was lost. A day or two after, the body of the *patron* was washed ashore, and the fact was reported to the *gen d'arme* of the place, who, according to French law, proceeded to make his official inquest. In the group which gathered around the ghastly object stretched out upon the beach—the tall soldier wrapped in official dignity, with note-book in hand taking down the testimony of the excited fisherfolk, men, women, and children, one old man pointing with long finger to where *it* had come out of the sea—in this awe-stricken group, with the towering cliffs behind, the artist found the element of dramatic interest which supplied the story for the picture."

Mr. Reinhart is one of the founders of the New York Etching Club and the Tile Club, and a member of the Water-Color Society and the Society of American Artists. He has done much work as an illustrator of books, and an artist in journalism. He traveled in Spain with George Parsons Lathrop, and made the beautiful drawings in that author's "Spanish Vistas." For a number of years he has been a resident of Paris and a contributor to the *Salon*. Among his recompenses are his *Mention Honorable* at the *Salon* of 1887; the second medal at the Exposition at Sydney, Australia, in the same year; the first gold medal at Philadelphia in 1888; and the first medal for drawing, and the second medal for paint-

ing, at Paris in 1889. To him, as to Mr. Lowell, the world of the imagination is "not the world of abstraction and nonentity, as some conceive, but a world formed out of chaos by a sense of the beauty that is in man and the earth on which he dwells."

GUY F. MAYNARD · *A Woman of Holland.*

This same idea is expressed by a foreign critic in a review of a picture of Ellen Terry by Mr. John S. Sargent, who took one of the two Medals of Honor in the American department of the fine arts at the Paris Exposition of 1889; and the words are significant as showing the esteem in which our brightest young countrymen are now held in Europe: "To call Mr. Sargent's picture of Ellen Terry a portrait would be to misname this remarkable *tour de force.* It is an artistic impression, using the word correctly, of the actress's dramatic personality, as on the stage she flashes before one out of the darkness, in her heavy coils and folds of glittering green and blue drapery, lustrous as a serpent's skin, her ruddy plaits of hair falling from either side the white face, with its red mouth and shining mesmeric eyes, as she holds the regal coronet above her head. It is a wonderful study, this, concentrating in one attitude and impression the whole dramatic conception of the character; especially striking for the mastery of the painting, and the astonishing and splendid harmonies of the draperies. It would seem that the painter has here found a subject absolutely congenial to him."

Before closing this volume, it is pertinent to observe that at least one of the formative forces of the present art-epoch has had scarcely any appreciable influence upon our younger American painters. This force is Impressionism. But, what is Impressionism? An answer to the much-disputed question was recently given to me by a representative Impressionist substantially as follows: The first exhibition of Impressionist pictures was made in Paris by M. Durand-Ruel, in 1872, with the works of Monet, Renoir, Pissarro, Sisley, and others; but the Impressionists themselves claim that their method of painting was practiced by the Greeks, by the pre-Raphaelites, and, to some extent, by Turner and by Delacroix; that the Turks four hundred years ago used it in tapestries, and that Japanese painting, though crude, derives its harmony from it. As long ago as 1830, they say, Chevreuil demonstrated the theory in his well-known book on color; and it is only ignorance that sneers at Impressionism as a new discovery by a set of conceited iconoclasts. In the pictures by Giotto, Fra Angelico, and Botticelli, particularly, does pre-Raphaelitism show itself to be Impressionistic—that is to say, these artists were governed by the two leading principles of Impressionism, namely, "Don't mix your pigments," and "Study the complementaries." The first of these principles refers to the practice of using the pigments in the condition in which they are when squeezed out of the tubes; whereas, most painters mix them on a palette before transferring them to canvas. Every person who has seen an Impressionist picture will remember that its pigments represent the simple and primitive colors. The second of these principles refers to the practice of depending upon the effect of the juxtaposition

of pigments, each pigment having its own proper complementary, which modifies its force when placed next to it. The result of the application of these principles is a greater luminosity than is obtained by the usual methods—a luminosity so great that the art-dealers are afraid to hang a landscape by Monet in the same room with a landscape by a non-Impressionist, even by so famous a painter as Rousseau or Corot, because the latter seems to have all the life and brilliancy

RIDGWAY KNIGHT : *The Noonday Rest.*

taken out of it. Mr. Fuller, a well-known collector in New York city, has two Monets hanging in one of his galleries, which cause all the pictures around it to look dark and faded ; and there is not a single canvas by a member of the celebrated Fontainebleau school which would not lose in luminosity when placed beside a canvas by Monet, Renoir, Pissarro, or Sisley. So fundamental a quality with the Impressionists is luminosity that sometimes they are called the Illuminists. The more common name, " Impressionists," was given to them in derision, but they have accepted it, all the same.

Judged, therefore, by this standard of luminosity, the Fontainebleau school (of which so extraordinary and satisfying an exhibition was made in the American

Art Galleries, New York city, in the autumn of 1889, in connection with a collection of the bronzes and water-colors of Barye) is not remarkable at all.   Corot
has more luminosity than any other member of it, but he has, comparatively, only
a little, while Millet has none, and Diaz has none, and Rousseau has none, and
Jules Dupré has absolutely none.   In fact, the disastrous mistake of the Fontainebleau school was (say the Impressionists) in taking their inspiration from Constable,
instead of from Turner; for, although Turner was by no means a representative
Impressionist, he nevertheless had the instinct of Impressionism, as is seen by his
manner of separating his pigments on his canvas.   If he had only refrained from
mixing them on his palette, and if, in addition, he had paid due attention to the
complementaries—that is, to the influence of one pigment upon another next to
it—he would have ranked as a leader of Impressionism.   When Giotto puts a
green gown on the Virgin, he always juxtaposes something red.   Why?   Because
he respects the complementaries.   And it is in mastering the science of the complementaries—as laid down by Chevreuil, Rood, and others—that the difficulty of
learning Impressionism consists.   A student can acquire in five minutes the method
of execution, if he has been drilled in the science of drawing; but it takes a long
time to comprehend the theory of the complementaries.

     At the École des Beaux-Arts they certainly do not learn it.   What they are
taught is, a *way* of drawing, a *way* of coloring—namely, the pseudo-classic way
of their teachers, who say to their pupils, "You must make a nose so, because
the Greeks made it so."   Hence, all their noses are alike.   Those who possess the
true instinct are compelled to forget all that they learned at the École des Beaux-
Arts; for the really classic way to learn to draw is to observe Nature; the best
way to study art is to study Nature, to find a way for ourselves by observation.
Of course, we must have a science of the subject, but this should be acquired by
children at school, who should learn to draw as they learn to write, and should
be taught Chevreuil and Rood as they are taught arithmetic and spelling.   But in
most of our art-training we are the slaves of tradition.   A painting should be
seen, as Nature is seen, at a distance sufficient to allow its colors to blend; or,
generally speaking, at a distance as long as three times its diagonal.   But most
amateurs want to stand near enough to smell the paint.   Dupré once tried for
three months to make a true study from Nature.   He could not do it; it was
too difficult.   Therefore he painted "compositions," and his only merit is a certain
pleasantness of composition.   Do you see Nature in his pictures—in his black
shadows under a blue sky?   And his drawing is not good, either.   Fortuny had
luminosity without harmony; it was a discordant luminosity, because he relied for

S. W. GRIGGS : *Still Life*

his effect upon the mixing of pigments, instead of upon their juxtaposition. Titian had luminosity, but less than the pre-Raphaelites. Leonardo was less luminous than Veronese, but greater in drawing. Raphael's painting, as painting, is not worth looking at. The Impressionists wish to be moderns—to study what they see in Nature more than anything else. The difference between them and their contemporaries is a difference of method. With their method they can perfectly well make a painting out of Nature. But this method is essential.

Such is Impressionism as it was described to me one afternoon, during a walk through the Louvre, by the venerable M. Pissarro, a leader of the school. I have neither the space nor the inclination to discuss the subject here. My purpose has been, by describing Impressionism—a term which so few persons understand—to show that, in its characteristic tenets, it has no disciples among the authors of these RECENT IDEALS OF AMERICAN ART.

OGDEN Wood. *In the Dunes*